YESHUSTAN
Living A Heavenly Life

DR. ABHIJIT DIP

BLUEROSE PUBLISHERS
India | U.K.

Copyright © Dr Abhijit Dip 2024

All rights reserved by author. No part of this publication may be reproduced, stored in a retrieval system or transmitted in any form or by any means, electronic, mechanical, photocopying, recording or otherwise, without the prior permission of the author. Although every precaution has been taken to verify the accuracy of the information contained herein, the publisher assumes no responsibility for any errors or omissions. No liability is assumed for damages that may result from the use of information contained within.

BlueRose Publishers takes no responsibility for any damages, losses, or liabilities that may arise from the use or misuse of the information, products, or services provided in this publication.

For permissions requests or inquiries regarding this publication, please contact:

BLUEROSE PUBLISHERS
www.BlueRoseONE.com
info@bluerosepublishers.com
+91 8882 898 898
+4407342408967

ISBN: 978-93-5989-019-7

Cover design: Rishav Rai
Typesetting: Rohit

First Edition: February 2024

Yeshustan – Living A Heavenly Life

Yeshustan is the place where we belong to Jesus, and Jesus is our King. The name is derived from the Persian suffix "-stān," which means "place of.", Kabulistan means the place of Kabuls, Afghanistan means the place of the Afghans. In the same way, Yeshustan is the place where we, as Christians, belong to Jesus, and we live for Him. Yeshustan is the exisence of my soul.

Yeshustan is not just a physical place but rather a state of being where Jesus is recognized as our King and we belong to Him. It is a concept that encompasses both a spiritual and a physical reality, where our relationship with Jesus is central to our existence. According to the Bible, Jesus Himself said that He would come again to take us with Him so that we can be where He is (John 14:3 - NLT). Additionally, in Revelation 11:15 (NLT), it states that the world will become the Kingdom of our Lord and of His Christ, and He will reign forever and ever.

The idea of Yeshustan is not just a theological concept, but it is a belief system that shapes the way we live our lives. As Christians, we recognize that we are not just citizens of this world, but we also belong to the Kingdom of God, which is led by Jesus Christ. Therefore, we strive to live our lives in accordance with His teachings and His example, with the hope of one day entering into His presence.

The term Yeshustan is not found in the Bible, but it is a term that has been used to describe a world where Jesus is recognized as

King, and His followers are part of His Kingdom. It is a place of peace, love, and joy, where God's will is done, and His presence is felt by all. In essence, Yeshustan is a vision of a world that is free from the sin and corruption that plagues our current world, and it is a hope that we hold onto as we await the return of Jesus Christ.

We Belong to Jesus:

In the sacred tapestry of our Christian narrative, an unshakable truth resonates — we belong to Jesus. Our foundational creed finds roots in the timeless verses of the Bible, where the echo of Romans 14:8 (ESV) reverberates: "For if we live, we live to the Lord, and if we die, we die to the Lord. Hence, whether we live or whether we die, we are the Lord's." This profound declaration etches upon the Christian heart a fundamental reality — our lives cease to be self-contained entities; they are now intricately interwoven with the divine.

Galatians 2:20 (ESV) amplifies this truth as the apostle Paul, with pen and parchment, inscribes the crucifixion of the old self with Christ. The demise of the sin-enslaved being births forth a new existence, a life defined by unwavering faith in the Son of God, who, in profound love, sacrificed Himself for our redemption. This reborn life is not a mere existence; it is a journey co-authored by Jesus, who, through His Holy Spirit, takes residence within us.

A glimpse into Revelation 21:3 (ESV) unfurls the canvas of a future reality — a divine union where God, in intimate communion, dwells among His people, and they become His, embraced by the very presence of their God. This vision extends beyond the temporal; it underscores our dual existence as not merely physical entities but spiritual beings, meticulously crafted in the divine image, destined for communion with our Creator.

The profound belief that we belong to Jesus echoes through the corridors of our lives, inviting us to transcend self-interest and mundane desires. It is a summons to embody the very character of Jesus — to love sacrificially, to be conduits of His grace, and to herald the message of salvation to a world ensnared in darkness.

This belief isn't a theological abstraction; it's a living reality that shapes the contours of our existence. We were conceived for communion with God, and our restless hearts find solace only in Him. Therefore, let us not merely acknowledge but fervently embrace the profound truth — we belong to Jesus. And in the tapestry of our lives, let every thread and hue be woven in a symphony that honors Him and resounds with the majestic glory of His name.

Jesus is Our King:

In the tapestry of our Christian faith, Jesus stands as the unrivaled King, a truth woven into the sacred fabric of our beliefs by the very words of the Bible. It foretells a time when Christ, at the divine orchestration of the Almighty God, shall be unveiled from the heavens, the King of all kings and Lord of all lords (1 Timothy 6:15 - NLT). This prophetic pronouncement transcends mere kingship; it heralds Jesus as the sovereign ruler over the entirety of creation, His dominion extending beyond earthly realms.

To fathom the depth of what it means for Jesus to be our King, we turn to Romans 14:8 (ESV), unveiling a profound reality: "For if we live, we live to the Lord, and if we die, we die to the Lord. So then, whether we live or whether we die, we are the Lord's." This scripture affirms a fundamental truth — our lives, as

Christians, are not self-contained but are intricately entwined with Jesus, our Lord and King.

Under the benevolent rule of Jesus, our lives cease to be compartmentalized fragments; instead, every facet falls under His sovereign gaze. His kingship extends beyond our spiritual journey to embrace the entirety of our being — the physical, emotional, and mental. In the eloquence of Matthew 6:25-34, Jesus beckons us to cast our cares upon Him, assuring us of His providence.

Yet, Jesus as our King is not merely an affirmation of His concern for our individual well-being; it's a royal summons to partake in His grand mission — the establishment of the Kingdom of God on earth. He invites us to embody His love, grace, and truth, and to be ambassadors of His redemptive message in a world yearning for hope, healing, and restoration.

The journey under the reign of Jesus, though marked by challenges and even persecution, is anchored in the triumphant assurance that our King has conquered the world (John 16:33). His abiding promise resonates through the ages, "I am with you always, to the end of the age" (Matthew 28:20).

In the grand tapestry of our faith, Jesus emerges not merely as a King but as our King. His dominion blankets creation, and His reign touches every nuance of our existence. As Christians, we are beckoned to submit to His lordship, to actively engage in His redemptive mission, and to be living testimonies reflecting His love, grace, and truth to a world ensnared in darkness. Let us, therefore, embrace this profound truth — Jesus is not just a King; He is our King, and may our lives resound with His eternal glory.

Live Like and For Jesus:

Living like and for Jesus is not merely a spiritual suggestion but a divine mandate echoing through the corridors of Scripture. Ephesians 5:1-2 (NLT) resounds this call, urging believers to "Imitate God, therefore, in everything you do, because you are His dear children. Live a life filled with love, following the example of Christ."

This divine injunction requires us to mirror Jesus not only in our actions but in our values, priorities, and attitudes. It beckons us to sacrificially love others, forgive as we've been forgiven, and generously share our time, talents, and resources — echoing the very essence of Christ's earthly journey.

Yet, living for Jesus transcends imitation; it's a surrender of our entire lives, making Him the focal point of every endeavor. Philippians 1:20-26 (NLT) encapsulates this truth, declaring, "For to me, living means living for Christ, and dying is even better... I trust that my life will bring honor to Christ, whether I live or die."

In this divine calling, every aspect of our lives becomes an opportunity to honor Christ. It impels us to employ our talents in His service, extending love as Christ did, and embodying a living testimony of His transformative love and grace.

In my personal journey, this mandate took root at the tender age of 17 when, inspired by a fervent desire to serve Christ, I founded "Life For Christ Ministry." What began as a humble endeavor has blossomed into a movement touching the lives of over 500,000 souls across more than five countries. It stands as a testament to the enduring impact of living for Jesus.

Undoubtedly, the path of imitating and living for Jesus is fraught with challenges, trials, and even persecution. Yet, our solace lies in the assurance that Jesus has conquered the world (John 16:33) and promises His abiding presence till the end of the age (Matthew 28:20).

As we navigate this divine call, let us not forget that we belong to Jesus. His indwelling spirit empowers us to lead lives that resonate with sacrificial love, mirroring His example. May our existence be a testament to His love and grace, inviting others to encounter the transformative power of a life lived for Jesus.

Prologue

As devoted followers of Jesus, our calling is profound—we are summoned to live our lives in dedication to Him, to embrace His love and extend it to others, and to carry His transformative message to a world in desperate need.

Amidst the complexities and trials of our earthly journey, there exists an opportunity to savor a glimpse of heaven. This is achievable by adopting a lifestyle that mirrors Jesus, one that encompasses both love for Him and love for others, transcending the challenges of our daily existence.

In the face of skepticism, some may question the commitment of Indian Christians, branding them as "rice bag Christians" in a derogatory manner, insinuating that they traded their former faith for material gain. When confronted with such inquiries, my response is simple: I am a Christian because I understand my origin, comprehend my purpose, and have clarity about my destination. This book, Yeshustan, is poised to offer you a similar revelation.

By delving into its pages, you will embark on a journey that elucidates the profound reasons behind our faith. You will discover a narrative that transcends mere religious labels, providing a meaningful exploration of the deeper dimensions of belief. Yeshustan has the potential to be a guiding light, illuminating the path to understanding your roots, purpose, and ultimate destination.

As Christians, we are called to live a life that is set apart for God, a life that reflects the love, grace, and mercy of our Lord Jesus Christ. This life is not just about going to church or following certain religious rituals, but it is a way of living that permeates every aspect of our existence. In Romans 12, the apostle Paul provides us with a blueprint for this heavenly lifestyle, a lifestyle that is both practical and transformative.

Renew Your Mind:

The first step in living a heavenly lifestyle is to renew your mind. Paul says in Romans 12:2, "Do not conform to the pattern of this world, but be transformed by the renewing of your mind. Then you will be able to test and approve what God's will is—his good, pleasing and perfect will." This means that we need to change the way we think about ourselves, about others, and about the world around us. We need to align our thoughts with God's thoughts, and this can only happen when we spend time in His Word, in prayer, and in fellowship with other believers.

Use Your Gifts:

The next step in living a heavenly lifestyle is to use your gifts. Paul says in Romans 12:6-8, "We have different gifts, according to the grace given to each of us. If your gift is prophesying, then prophesy in accordance with your faith; if it is serving, then serve; if it is teaching, then teach; if it is to encourage, then give encouragement; if it is giving, then give generously; if it is to lead, do it diligently; if it is to show mercy, do it cheerfully." This means that we need to identify the gifts that God has given us and use them to serve others. We are not called to live for ourselves but to live for others, just as Christ did.

Love One Another:

The third step in living a heavenly lifestyle is to love one another. Paul says in Romans 12:9-10, "Love must be sincere. Hate what is evil; cling to what is good. Be devoted to one another in love. Honor one another above yourselves." This means that we need to love others with the same love that Christ has for us. We need to put aside our own interests and desires and prioritize the needs of others. This kind of love is not just an emotion, but it is a choice that we make every day.

Overcome Evil with Good:

The fourth and final step in living a heavenly lifestyle is to overcome evil with good. Paul says in Romans 12:21, "Do not be overcome by evil, but overcome evil with good." This means that we need to resist the temptation to retaliate when we are wronged, but instead, we need to respond with kindness, forgiveness, and compassion. This is not an easy thing to do, but it is possible with the help of the Holy Spirit.

Living a heavenly lifestyle is not about being perfect, but it is about being transformed by the renewing of our minds, using our gifts to serve others, loving one another, and overcoming evil with good.

Yeshustan is a state of being where we belong to Jesus and live for Him, and this kind of life is both practical and transformative. As we delve into the pages of this book, let us open our hearts and minds to the transforming power of God's Word, and let us allow His Spirit to guide us into a life that is truly heavenly.

In this book I want to give you an insight about living a heavenly life while living on this earth and for that we have to know God and know our role here as we continue our journey to our eternal home, Just as a glimpse I am mentioning just a preface of all the chapters here.

1. Chapter 1: Revealing the Divine: Exploring God's Nature and Attributes

Chapter 1 of this book explores the nature and attributes of God. It explains how God is revealed in the Bible and how His character is manifested in the world around us. It also examines some of the philosophical and theological arguments for the existence of God.

2. Chapter 2: The Savior's Story: Why Jesus ?

Chapter 2 focuses on Jesus Christ, the Son of God. It explores His life, teachings, death, and resurrection, and the significance of these events for humanity. It also looks at the role that Jesus plays in our lives as our Lord and Savior, and how we can have a personal relationship with Him.

3. Chapter 3: The Beginning of It All: Understanding the Story of Adam and Eve

Chapter 3 takes a closer look at the story of Adam and Eve, the first human beings created by God. It explores the creation account in the book of Genesis, and how the sin of Adam and Eve had far-reaching consequences for humanity.

4. Chapter 4: The Dilemma of Disobedience: Delving into the Concept of Sin

Chapter 4 examines the concept of sin, which is the disobedience of God's commands. It looks at the effects of sin on individuals and society, and the consequences of sin in both this life and the next.

5. Chapter 5: From Sin to Salvation: Embracing the Path to Redemption

Chapter 5 discusses the concept of salvation, which is the forgiveness of sins and the restoration of our relationship with God through faith in Jesus Christ. It explores the different aspects of salvation, including justification, sanctification, and glorification.

6. Chapter 6: The Guiding Spirit: Understanding the Role of the Holy Spirit

Chapter 6 focuses on the Holy Spirit, the third person of the Trinity. It explores the role of the Holy Spirit in the lives of Christians, including sanctification, empowerment, and guidance.

7. Chapter 7: Conversing with the Divine: The Power and Importance of Prayer

Chapter 7 looks at the importance of prayer in the Christian life. It explores different types of prayer, the benefits of prayer, and how to pray effectively.

8. Chapter 8: Fasting for Spiritual Growth: Harnessing the Power of Abstinence

Chapter 8 discusses the power of fasting, which is the practice of abstaining from food for spiritual purposes. It explores the different types of fasting, the benefits of fasting, and how to fast effectively.

9. Chapter 9: The Freedom of Forgiveness: Unlocking Its Healing Power

Chapter 9 explores the power of forgiveness, which is a key aspect of the Christian faith. It looks at what forgiveness is, why it is important, and how to forgive others.

10. Chapter 10: Building Christian Families: Biblical Principles of A Family

Chapter 10 focuses on the power of Christian family, which is a vital part of the church and the Kingdom of God. It explores the biblical principles of marriage, parenting, and family life.

11. Chapter 11: From Death to Life: Exploring the Hope of Resurrection

Chapter 11 discusses death and the power of resurrection, which is a central aspect of the Christian faith. It explores what happens after we die, the hope of resurrection, and the significance of the resurrection of Jesus Christ.

12. Chapter 12: The Joy of Giving: Unleashing the Power of Generosity

Chapter 12 looks at the power of giving, which is a key aspect of Christian stewardship. It explores the biblical principles of giving, the benefits of giving, and how to give generously.

13. Chapter 13: A Glimpse of the Eternal Home: The Biblical Vision of the Future

Finally, Chapter 13 explores the concept of the earth and the eternal home, which is the hope of the Christian faith. It looks at the biblical vision of the future, including the new heavens and the new earth, and the ultimate triumph of God's Kingdom.

Overall, this book seeks to provide a comprehensive exploration of the Christian faith, from the nature of God to the hope of eternal life. It is intended to deepen the faith of believers, and to provide a clear and compelling introduction to those who are seeking to understand the Christian faith.

About The Author

Dr. Abhijit Kumar Dip is an exceptional individual, celebrated for his unwavering commitment to the service of others. Hailing from the quaint town of Balangir in Odisha, he embarked on an educational journey that would eventually shape his path of service. Dr. Dip's academic voyage led him to Buntain Theological College (Assembly of God Church) in Kolkata, where he earned his Bachelor's degree in theology. His thirst for knowledge and dedication to his calling continued, culminating in a Master's in Divinity from Berean College in Andhra Pradesh. In recognition of his remarkable contributions to his field, Berean College honored him with an Honorary Doctorate (Doctor of Divinity) in October 2018.

Dr. Dip's unyielding passion for serving others ignited a remarkable journey of ministry. At a tender age of 19, he founded "LIFE FOR CHRIST MINISTRIES" and has since been at the helm as its founder and director. His altruistic spirit also led him to serve as the Odisha state representative of the Good News Centre in New Delhi, as well as the program coordinator for Good News Health Care Services. In 2019, his relentless dedication bore fruit as he successfully expanded his ministry to an international scale, renaming it as "LIFE FOR CHRIST INTERNATIONAL MINISTRIES."

On a global stage, Dr. Dip's dedication to humanity has garnered well-deserved recognition. He was conferred with the

"MAHATMA GANDHI INTERNATIONAL PEACE AWARD" by the All India Congress Social Organisation in 2019 and was bestowed the title of Man of Divinity by the International UNICEF Council in 2020. His diverse initiatives have spanned areas such as women and child welfare, youth empowerment, ensuring the nourishment of the underprivileged, and delivering vital healthcare services.

In the face of profound personal tragedy, when he lost his father to the clutches of COVID-19 in April 2021, Dr. Dip exemplified unwavering resilience. With renewed determination, he continued to embrace his God-given mission, exemplifying an indomitable spirit. In 2021, he took yet another visionary step, founding A.D.A.M.S (Abhijit Dip and Associates for Management And Solutions), a business with a noble mission. This initiative is geared towards fostering self-sufficiency among churches and ministries in India, offering them a path to independence. Additionally, Dr. Dip plays an integral role in Purple Microgift, a project dedicated to empowering vulnerable and underprivileged women in India through small-scale business ventures. He also serves as the Director of Resources Asia for Bridge Consulting USA, a mission aimed at creating an enriching working environment for software developers in India.

Furthermore, Dr. Dip selflessly serves as the state secretary for ALL INDIA CONGRESS COMMITTEE MINORITY DEPARTMENT. In this role, he passionately advocates for the rights and welfare of Christians in India, particularly in the face of rising persecution. His dedication to this cause is a testament to his unwavering commitment to his faith and his fellow believers.

As the author of "Yeshustan," Dr. Dip brings to his writing an extensive wealth of experience, as well as a steadfast commitment to service. His words on the page carry the same revolutionary vision and admirable determination that have defined his life's work, offering inspiration and motivation to all who have the privilege of reading his words.

Contents

1. Revealing the Divine: Exploring God's Nature and Attributes 1
2. The Savior's Story: Why Jesus ? 11
3. The Beginning of It All: Understanding the Story of Adam and Eve 41
4. The Dilemma of Disobedience: Delving into the Concept of Sin 49
5. From Sin to Salvation: Embracing the Path to Redemption. 62
6. The Guiding Spirit: Understanding the Role of the Holy Spirit 81
7. Conversing with the Divine: The Power and Importance of Prayer 89
8. Fasting for Spiritual Growth: Harnessing the Power of Abstinence 100
9. The Freedom of Forgiveness: Unlocking Its Healing Power 109
10. Building Christian Families: Biblical Principles of a Family 117
11. From Death to Life: Exploring the Hope of Resurrection 131
12. The Joy of Giving: Unleashing the Power of Generosity 135
13. A Glimpse of the Eternal Home: The Biblical Vision of the Future... 141

Chapter 1

Revealing the Divine: Exploring God's Nature and Attributes

In the tapestry of my upbringing in India, where reverence for a multitude of gods and goddesses was woven into the very fabric of life, my spiritual journey began. It was a quest born out of the rich soil of a land that worshipped more deities than one could fathom, sparking in me an insatiable urge to unravel the mysteries and find the real God. Yeshustan, the opening chapter of the Bible, became my guiding light, illuminating the path to a profound understanding of the nature of God and the origins of existence.

As I navigated the complexities of a cultural landscape adorned with myriad beliefs, the words of Jesus in John 17:3 resonated within me: "Now this is eternal life: that they know you, the only true God, and Jesus Christ, whom you have sent." In a land where spiritual diversity adorned every corner, the pursuit of knowing the true God wasn't just a preference but the very essence of eternal life.

Yeshustan, with its timeless narrative, went beyond being a mere reflection; it became a personal revelation. The creation story, beginning with "In the beginning," transcended cultural boundaries, offering a foundational truth that spoke directly to the chaos of diverse beliefs surrounding me. The unfolding narrative revealed a God who brought order to disorder, infusing purpose into every thread of creation.

Yeshustan wasn't confined to the pages of an ancient text; it was an invitation to intimately encounter the divine. "God saw everything that he had made, and indeed, it was very good." These words reverberated not just on parchment but in the vibrant hues of India, in the bustling streets, and in the faces that mirrored the artistry of the Creator.

Amidst a land where spirituality saturated the air, Yeshustan became my compass, guiding me through the labyrinth of myriad gods to find the One who was both transcendent and immanent. The narrative showcased the power and wisdom displayed in creation, affirming the God I sought, while His love and grace permeated every aspect of life.

My journey toward knowing God became a profoundly personal one through the pages of Yeshustan. It wasn't just theological exploration; it was the story of a seeker in a land of myriad beliefs, finding the anchor of truth. As the themes unfolded, I discovered not only who God is but also how to authentically live in a profound relationship with Him. Yeshustan, to me, became a testament to the universality of truth, cutting through the cultural tapestry to reveal the God who is, and always was, the only true God.

As Christians, our faith is based on the belief in a personal and loving God who desires to have a relationship with us. Knowing God is the foundation of our faith and shapes our understanding of the world around us. In this chapter, we will explore the importance of knowing God and how we can deepen our relationship with Him.

The concept of the Trinity is a foundational belief of Christianity, and it has been a topic of debate and discussion for centuries. The doctrine of the Trinity teaches that there is one God who exists as three distinct Persons: the Father, the Son (Jesus Christ), and the Holy Spirit. This means that God is one in essence, yet three in Person. Each of these Persons is fully God, and yet there is only one God.

The doctrine of the Trinity expresses three crucial truths that are central to the Christian faith. Firstly, it affirms that the Father, Son, and Holy Spirit are distinct Persons. Each of these Persons has their own unique characteristics, yet they are united in their divine essence. This means that the Father is not the Son, and the Son is not the Holy Spirit, but each Person is fully God.

Secondly, the doctrine of the Trinity teaches that each of these Persons is fully God. This means that the Father is God, the Son is God, and the Holy Spirit is God. Each Person possesses all of the attributes of deity, such as omniscience, omnipotence, and omnipresence. The Son, Jesus Christ, is not a lesser God or a created being, but is equal in nature and essence to the Father and the Holy Spirit.

Thirdly, the doctrine of the Trinity affirms that there is only one God. Despite the fact that there are three distinct Persons in the Godhead, they are united in their divine essence and are not three separate Gods. This means that the Father, Son, and Holy Spirit are all equally God, and there is no hierarchy or subordination among them.

The concept of the Trinity is often difficult for people to understand, and it has been the subject of much debate and controversy throughout history. However, it is a fundamental belief of Christianity, and it serves as a reminder of the infinite complexity and beauty of God's nature.

The Trinity is not simply 1+1+1=3, but rather it is 1x1x1=1.

The concept of the Triune God, or the Holy Trinity, is one of the fundamental beliefs of Christianity. It states that there is one God who exists as three distinct persons: the Father, the Son (Jesus Christ), and the Holy Spirit. Each person of the Trinity has a unique role in the work of salvation.

The Father is the creator of all things and the source of all love, mercy, and grace. He sent his Son into the world to save humanity from sin and death. The Son willingly submitted to the Father's will and came to earth to live as a human being, suffer, and die on the cross as a sacrifice for our sins. Through his resurrection, he conquered death and offers eternal life to all who believe in him.

The Holy Spirit is the divine presence of God who dwells within believers. He empowers us to live a holy life, guides us in understanding and applying the truth of God's word, and intercedes for us in prayer.

The relationship between the three persons of the Trinity is one of perfect love and unity. They work together in perfect harmony to accomplish the work of salvation. The Son submits to the Father's will, and the Holy Spirit submits to both the Father and the Son. This submission is not a sign of inferiority or weakness but rather a reflection of the perfect love and unity that exists between them.

The baptism of Jesus provides a clear picture of the Triune God at work. The Father speaks from heaven, affirming his love for his Son. The Son is baptized in the Jordan River, identifying himself with sinful humanity, and the Holy Spirit descends upon him like a dove, empowering him for his ministry.

2 Corinthians 13:14 says, "May the grace of the Lord Jesus Christ, and the love of God, and the fellowship of the Holy Spirit be with you all." This verse acknowledges the distinct roles of each person of the Trinity while also emphasizing their unity and co-equality. It is a reminder that salvation is the work of the Triune God, and we can only experience it through faith in Jesus Christ.

Each of these Persons is fully God, yet they are not identical but have distinct roles in the work of redemption. Here are some key points to expand on this thought:

1. The Father as God: The Bible identifies the Father as God. Philippians 1:2 says, "Grace and peace to you from God our Father and the Lord Jesus Christ." The Father is the source of all creation and the ultimate authority in the Godhead. He is the one to whom Jesus prayed and submitted himself, and he is the one who sent the Holy Spirit to indwell believers.

2. Jesus as God: The New Testament explicitly identifies Jesus as God. Titus 2:13 says, "We wait for the blessed hope—the appearing of the glory of our great God and Savior, Jesus Christ." Jesus is fully God and fully human, having two distinct natures in one person. He is the second Person of the Trinity and the one who became incarnate, lived a sinless life, died on the cross as a substitute for sinners, and rose again from the dead.

3. Holy Spirit as God: The Holy Spirit is also identified as God in the Bible. Acts 5:3-4 says, "Then Peter said, 'Ananias, how is it that Satan has so filled your heart that you have lied to the Holy Spirit...You have not lied just to human beings but to God.'" The Holy Spirit is the third Person of the Trinity and is the one who

empowers believers for service, convicts of sin, and enables them to understand and apply God's truth.

4. Three distinct Persons: Although the Father, Son, and Holy Spirit are all fully God, they are distinct Persons. Each has a unique role in the work of redemption, and each is able to interact with the others in a personal way. The Father is not the Son or the Holy Spirit, the Son is not the Father or the Holy Spirit, and the Holy Spirit is not the Father or the Son. Yet, they are one in essence and purpose.

5. The unity of the Trinity: The doctrine of the Trinity emphasizes the unity of the three Persons of the Godhead. They are one in their love, their purpose, and their desire to save humanity. The Father loves the Son and the Holy Spirit, the Son loves the Father and the Holy Spirit, and the Holy Spirit loves the Father and the Son. Their unity is a reflection of their perfect love and their desire to redeem and restore all of creation.

The Bible affirms the doctrine of the Trinity, which teaches that there is one God who exists in three distinct Persons: the Father, the Son (Jesus Christ), and the Holy Spirit. This means that each Person is fully God, yet they are not identical, but have distinct roles in the work of redemption.

One way the Bible indicates the distinction between the Father, Son, and Holy Spirit is by their respective roles in salvation history. For example, John 3:16 says, "For God so loved the world that he gave his one and only Son, that whoever believes in him shall not perish but have eternal life." This verse shows that the Father sent the Son into the world to accomplish salvation for humanity. This indicates that the Father and the Son are distinct

Persons, because if the Father and the Son were the same person, there would be no need for one to send the other.

Furthermore, after the Son returned to the Father following his death and resurrection, the Father and the Son sent the Holy Spirit to the world. Jesus told his disciples in John 14:26, "But the Advocate, the Holy Spirit, whom the Father will send in my name, will teach you all things and will remind you of everything I have said to you." Acts 2:33 affirms this by stating, "Exalted to the right hand of God, he [Jesus] has received from the Father the promised Holy Spirit and has poured out what you now see and hear." These verses show that the Holy Spirit is distinct from the Father and the Son, as he is sent by both of them to carry out his work in the world.

In addition to their distinct roles in salvation history, the Father, Son, and Holy Spirit are also distinguished by their relationship to one another. The Father loves the Son, and the Son loves the Father (John 14:31). The Holy Spirit proceeds from the Father and the Son (John 15:26), indicating his unique relationship to both of them.

The baptism of Jesus is a key event in the New Testament that provides further evidence of the doctrine of the Trinity. In this event, the Father speaks from heaven, the Spirit descends from heaven in the form of a dove, and Jesus is baptized by John in the Jordan River (Mark 1:10-11).

The fact that the Father speaks from heaven indicates that he is a distinct Person from Jesus, who is being baptized, and from the Holy Spirit, who is descending in the form of a dove. This is consistent with the doctrine of the Trinity, which teaches that there is one God who exists in three distinct Persons.

Moreover, in John 1:1, it is affirmed that Jesus is God and, at the same time, that he was "with God," indicating that he is a distinct Person from God the Father. This verse emphasizes the dual nature of Jesus as both fully God and fully man.

In John 16:13-15, Jesus also speaks about the Holy Spirit as a distinct Person from the Father and the Son. He says that the Spirit will guide his disciples into all truth and will not speak on his own authority but will only speak what he hears. This indicates that the Holy Spirit has a unique relationship with the Father and the Son and is a distinct Person in the Godhead.

The baptism of Jesus and several passages in the Gospel of John provide further evidence of the doctrine of the Trinity.

The doctrine of the Trinity teaches us that the Father, Son, and Holy Spirit are three distinct Persons who are all fully God. This means that the Father is not the Son, the Son is not the Holy Spirit, and the Holy Spirit is not the Father. They are not just different roles or manifestations of God, but rather distinct Persons who exist in a close unity and work together in the work of redemption.

However, while they are distinct Persons, there is only one God. This may seem like a paradox or a contradiction, but it is an essential aspect of the Christian faith. Scripture is clear that there is only one God, and this truth is emphasized repeatedly throughout the Old and New Testaments.

For example, in Isaiah 45:21-22, God declares, "There is no other God besides me, a righteous God and a Savior; there is none besides me. Turn to me and be saved, all the ends of the earth! For I am God, and there is no other." This passage emphasizes that there is only one God who is righteous and saves his people.

Other Old Testament passages also emphasize the oneness of God. Deuteronomy 4:35 declares, "To you it was shown, that you might know that the Lord is God; there is no other besides him." Similarly, in 1 Samuel 2:2, Hannah praises God by saying, "There is none holy like the Lord; there is none besides you; there is no rock like our God."

In the New Testament, the oneness of God is also emphasized. In Mark 12:29, Jesus quotes the Shema from Deuteronomy 6:4-5, saying, "Hear, O Israel: The Lord our God, the Lord is one." This passage emphasizes that there is only one God, and Jesus affirms this truth by quoting it.

The doctrine of the Trinity has a practical application to the way we approach God in prayer. The Bible teaches that we can come to God the Father through the Son and in the Holy Spirit. This means that our approach to God is always mediated by the Son and empowered by the Spirit.

Jesus taught His disciples to pray to the Father (Matthew 6:9). In doing so, He acknowledged the Father's supremacy as the first Person of the Trinity. But Jesus also taught that He is the way to the Father and that no one comes to the Father except through Him (John 14:6). This means that when we pray, we must do so through the mediation of the Son.

The Holy Spirit, as the third Person of the Trinity, empowers us to pray and intercedes for us when we don't know how to pray (Romans 8:26-27). The Spirit also helps us to know and understand the mind of God (1 Corinthians 2:10-11), which is essential for effective prayer.

Therefore, when we pray, we should be conscious of the Trinity and approach God the Father through the Son and in the power of the Holy Spirit. We should seek to be led by the Spirit, who helps us to pray according to God's will (Romans 8:27), and we should ask the Father to answer our prayers for the sake of the Son (John 14:13-14).

Ultimately, the doctrine of the Trinity teaches us that our relationship with God is not a solitary one. We are not alone in our prayers, but we are in fellowship with the tri-personal God. This realization should deepen our worship, our gratitude, and our trust in God, knowing that we are relating to a God who is Father, Son, and Holy Spirit.

Chapter 2

The Savior's Story: Why Jesus ?

The heartbeat of the Christian faith resonates in the person and work of Jesus Christ, an unchanging truth that has echoed through the corridors of time since the faith's inception. Growing up in a land where diverse beliefs painted the spiritual canvas, I found myself drawn to the profound claims of Jesus—claims that stretched beyond mere doctrine, embedding themselves in the very fabric of human history and culture.

This chapter is more than a theological exploration; it is a journey into the heartbeat of my faith, an intimate quest to unravel the profound importance of Jesus. His declarations as the Son of God and the Savior of the world aren't just historical footnotes but pivotal truths that have shaped the narrative of humanity. In the bustling tapestry of diverse cultures, I sought to understand why Jesus is not merely a religious figure but the cornerstone that has left an indelible mark on the world.

The claims of Jesus, audacious as they may seem, became the foundation of my beliefs. This chapter, as personal as a conversation with a trusted friend, delves into the reasons why Jesus is paramount in my life. It's not a detached examination but an intimate exploration of His teachings, a journey into the impact that resonates far beyond theological doctrines.

His life, His death, and the enigma of His resurrection aren't just events of antiquity; they are the very keystones of my salvation. In a world teeming with questions, understanding the person and work of Jesus has become my compass, shaping the contours of my relationship with God. It's a journey that every Christian must embark upon, for in the intricacies of Jesus' life, we discover the bedrock of our faith.

Studying the life and teachings of Jesus goes beyond academic pursuit; it's a profound encounter with God's love and His intricate plan for humanity. In this chapter, I invite you not just to explore historical narratives but to walk alongside me in discovering the hope and assurance that spring forth from truly knowing Jesus. For me, this journey has been transformative, and I believe it holds the same promise for every seeker who dares to delve into the profound mystery of the person and work of Jesus Christ.

The person and work of Jesus Christ have been central to the Christian faith since its inception. Jesus' claims to be the Son of God and the Savior of the world are not only foundational to Christian belief but have also had a profound impact on human history and culture. In this chapter, we will delve into the reasons why Jesus is so important and examine the evidence for His claims. We will explore His teachings and the impact they have had on the world, as well as the significance of His life, death, and resurrection for our salvation. Understanding the person and work of Jesus is crucial for every Christian, as it forms the basis of our faith and shapes our relationship with God. By studying Jesus' life and teachings, we can deepen our understanding of God's love and plan for humanity, and find the hope and assurance that comes from knowing Him.

THE GOOD NEWS - Jesus is the good news of salvation, known as the gospel, is centred on the person and work of Jesus Christ. This gospel message is first hinted at in the Bible's opening chapters, where we find the story of Adam and Eve's sin in the Garden of Eden. In Genesis 3:15, God pronounces a curse on the serpent that deceived Eve, but also gives a promise of hope: "I will put enmity between you and the woman, and between your offspring and her offspring; he shall bruise your head, and you shall bruise his heel." This promise, known as the ***protoevangelium*** or "first gospel," contains the first mention of the good news of salvation in the Bible.

The promise of a Savior who would crush the head of the serpent became a central theme throughout the Old Testament. The prophets foretold of a coming Messiah who would rescue God's people from sin and death. And in the New Testament, we see the fulfillment of these prophecies in the person of Jesus Christ.

Jesus is the good news because He is the fulfillment of God's promise of salvation. He is the Son of God who came to earth, lived a sinless life, and died on the cross as a sacrifice for our sins. Through His death and resurrection, He conquered sin and death and offers eternal life to all who believe in Him. This is why Jesus is so important - He is the way, the truth, and the life, and no one can come to the Father except through Him (John 14:6).

THE BRIDGE - Jesus is often referred to as the bridge or mediator between God and humanity. The Bible teaches that due to sin, there is a separation between God and humanity (Isaiah 59:2). However, Jesus came to reconcile us to God and to bridge the gap caused by sin.

In John 14:6, Jesus Himself declared, "I am the way and the truth and the life. No one comes to the Father except through me." Through His death and resurrection, Jesus provided a way for us to be reconciled to God and to have eternal life. This is why He is often referred to as the bridge between God and humanity.

As believers, we are called to have faith in Jesus and to trust in His work on the cross for our salvation. Through Him, we can have a restored relationship with God and the hope of eternal life.

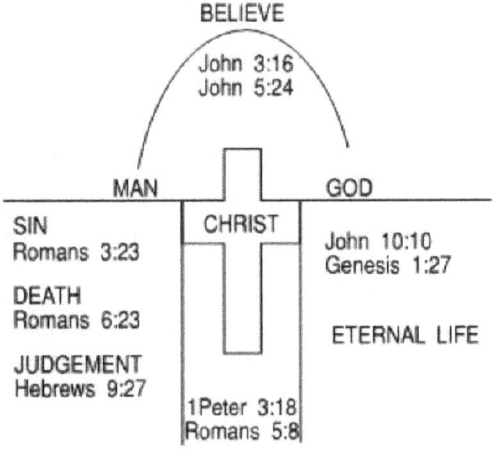

Yes, that's a great way to describe Jesus' role in our salvation. The Bible teaches that because of sin, there is a separation between God and humanity (Isaiah 59:2). But Jesus bridges that gap by reconciling us to God through His death and resurrection (2 Corinthians 5:18-19). He offers us salvation by taking the punishment for our sins and giving us His righteousness (Romans 3:23-24; 6:23). Through faith in Him, we can be forgiven and reconciled to God, and have eternal life (John 3:16). So, Jesus is not only the bridge of reconciliation, but also the bridge of salvation.

THE LAST ADAM - The Bible teaches that all human beings are descendants of Adam, the first man created by God. However, due to Adam's sin, all human beings inherited a sinful nature, which results in separation from God and eternal death. But the good news is that God provided a solution to this problem through Jesus Christ, who is called the Last Adam in 1 Corinthians 15:45-48.

The Last Adam is a term used to describe Jesus Christ, who is the second man from heaven and the last man to be without a sin nature. In contrast to the first Adam, who brought sin and death into the world, the Last Adam brings life and righteousness. Jesus Christ, as the God-man, is uniquely qualified to be the suitable sacrifice for the sins of the world.

Romans 5:12-21 provides further insight into the Last Adam concept, showing the parallel between Adam and Christ. Just as Adam's sin brought death and condemnation to all, so Christ's righteousness brings life and justification to all who believe in Him. The passage explains that through one man's disobedience (Adam), many were made sinners, but through one man's obedience (Christ), many will be made righteous.

In his letter to the Corinthians, Paul explains that the first Adam was created as a natural, earthly being, while the Last Adam was a life-giving spirit. This means that Jesus' nature was both fully human and fully divine, able to offer Himself as the sacrifice for sin. As Paul writes in 2 Corinthians 5:17-21, Jesus, who knew no sin, became sin for us so that in Him we might become the righteousness of God.

The Last Adam is a crucial concept in the Christian faith, representing Jesus Christ's role as the solution to humanity's sin problem. Through His death and resurrection, He offers salvation and the opportunity for new life to all who put their faith in Him. As Romans 5:18 proclaims, "Consequently, just as one trespass resulted in condemnation for all people, so also one righteous act resulted in justification and life for all people."

JESUS 100% HUMAN

1. THAT HE WAS BORN OF A WOMAN —THE VIRGIN MARY.

The humanity of Jesus is a fundamental belief of the Christian faith. The Bible clearly teaches that Jesus was born of a woman, the Virgin Mary, and that He was fully human. The Gospel accounts attest to His birth, life, and ministry as a human being. Matthew 1:18-25 describes the circumstances of His birth and emphasizes His human lineage through Joseph. Luke's Gospel also details the humanity of Jesus, describing His growth and development as a child, His baptism, and His temptation in the wilderness (Luke 2:40-52; 3:21-23; 4:1-13).

The New Testament writers also attest to the human nature of Jesus. John 1:14 states, "The Word became flesh and made his dwelling among us." This passage highlights the incarnation, which means that Jesus took on human form and dwelt among us. Paul emphasizes the humanity of Jesus in Romans 1:3, stating that Jesus was "born of the seed of David according to the flesh." Galatians 4:4 also affirms that Jesus was "born of a woman."

Jesus' humanity is significant for several reasons. First, it demonstrates God's love and compassion for humanity. Through becoming human, Jesus experienced first-hand the joys, sorrows, and challenges of human life. He can sympathize with our weaknesses and offer us comfort and hope (Hebrews 4:15-16).

Second, Jesus' humanity makes Him a suitable and compassionate high priest who can intercede on our behalf before God (Hebrews 2:17-18). Finally, Jesus' humanity is essential for our salvation. As a fully human being, Jesus was able to offer Himself as a perfect sacrifice for the sins of humanity (Hebrews 10:10-14).

In conclusion, the humanity of Jesus is a foundational belief of Christianity. Jesus was born of a woman, the Virgin Mary, and was fully human, experiencing the joys and sorrows of life on earth. This reality demonstrates God's love for humanity, makes Jesus a compassionate high priest, and is essential for our salvation.

2. HE GREW IN WISDOM AND STATURE AS OTHER HUMAN BEINGS DO. HE WAS SUBJECT TO THE ORDINARY LAWS OF HUMAN DEVELOPMENT INBODY AND SOUL.

Jesus was 100% human and experienced the full range of human development in body and soul. As mentioned in Luke 2:40 and 52, Jesus "grew in wisdom and stature," just like any other human being would. This means that He went through the natural process of physical and intellectual growth, which required time and effort.

Moreover, Luke 2:46 describes how Jesus was found in the temple, "sitting in the midst of the doctors, both hearing them, and asking them questions." This shows that even at a young age, Jesus was curious and seeking knowledge. He was eager to learn and understand more about God and the world around Him.

In addition to growing in wisdom, Jesus also grew in favor with God and man. This means that He developed a deep and meaningful relationship with God, and He was also able to form friendships and connections with other people.

Overall, the fact that Jesus grew and developed just like any other human being confirms His humanity. He experienced the same joys and struggles that we all face, and yet He was without sin (Hebrews 4:15). As a result, He can relate to us in a unique and powerful way, and we can find comfort in knowing that He understands our human experience.

3. HE HAD THE APPEARANCE OF A MAN.

Jesus is 100% human because He had the appearance of a man. As mentioned in John 4:9, Jesus was mistaken for an ordinary man when He spoke to the Samaritan woman at the well. Similarly, in Luke 24:13, two disciples on the road to Emmaus did not recognize Jesus as anything other than an ordinary man. Even after Jesus had risen from the dead, Mary Magdalene mistook Him for a gardener in John 20:15, and the disciples did not recognize Him at first when He appeared to them on the shore in John 21:4-5.

These accounts show that Jesus had a physical body like any other human being, with no distinguishing features that set Him apart from other men. He ate and drank, slept and rested, and experienced the same physical sensations as any other human being. He could be seen, heard, and touched, as evidenced by the numerous interactions He had with people throughout His ministry.

Moreover, the fact that Jesus had the appearance of a man is significant because it affirms His humanity. Jesus did not merely take on the appearance of a man, but He was fully and completely human in every way. This means that He experienced the full range of human emotions and physical sensations, including pain, hunger, thirst, joy, sorrow, and love.

In summary, the fact that people mistook Jesus for an ordinary man confirms His humanity. He had a physical body like any other human being, with no distinguishing features that set Him apart. He was fully and completely human in every way, and yet He was also fully and completely God. This is the mystery of the incarnation, and it is central to the Christian faith.

4. HE WAS POSSESSED OF A HUMAN PHYSICAL NATURE: BODY, SOUL AND SPIRIT.

Jesus is 100% human because He was possessed of a human physical nature, including a body, soul, and spirit. As John 1:14 says, "And the Word was made flesh," which means that Jesus took on a physical human body. Hebrews 2:14 also confirms this, stating that Jesus "also himself likewise took part of the same [flesh and blood]."

Moreover, the fact that Jesus had a human physical nature is evident in the way that He speaks about His body, soul, and spirit in the Gospels. In Matthew 26:12, for example, Jesus speaks of His body when He says, "She hath poured this ointment on my body." In verse 38, He speaks of His soul when He says, "My soul is exceeding sorrowful." And in Luke 23:46, Jesus speaks of His spirit when He says, "Father, into thy hands I commend my spirit."

Furthermore, in Luke 24:39, Jesus invites His disciples to touch Him and see that He has a physical body. He says, "Behold my hands and my feet, that it is I myself: handle me, and see; for a spirit hath not flesh and bones, as ye see me have." This shows that Jesus was not merely a spiritual entity or a ghost but had a physical body that could be seen, touched, and handled. Jesus' possession of a human physical nature, including a body, soul, and spirit, affirms His humanity. He was fully and completely human in every way, just like any other human being, and yet He was also fully and completely God. This is the mystery of the incarnation, and it is central to the Christian faith. The incarnation of Jesus Christ is the central doctrine of the Christian faith, which affirms that God took on human flesh and became fully and completely human while remaining fully divine. The doctrine of the incarnation holds that Jesus Christ came into possession of a real human nature when He was born of the Virgin Mary.

When we say that Jesus had a human nature, we mean that He was truly human in every sense of the word. He had a human body, a human soul, and a human spirit. He experienced hunger, thirst, fatigue, pain, and all the other physical limitations of being human. He also experienced the full range of human emotions, including joy, sorrow, and anger.

However, it is important to distinguish between a human nature and a carnal nature. A carnal nature is the result of sin and is not an integral part of humanity as God created it. In other words, it is not necessary for human beings to be sinful. Jesus' human nature was truly human, yet sinless. He was tempted in every way, just like we are, yet He never sinned (Hebrews 4:15).

By taking on human flesh, Jesus identified with humanity in a way that was unprecedented. He came not only to His own, but He came in the likeness of their own flesh. This means that He became fully and completely human, sharing in our joys and sorrows, our triumphs and failures, and our hopes and fears.

In summary, the incarnation of Jesus Christ affirms that God took on human flesh and became fully and completely human while remaining fully divine. By taking on a real human nature, Jesus identified with humanity in a way that was unprecedented, sharing in our joys and sorrows, our triumphs and failures, and our hopes and fears. And yet, He was sinless, making Him the perfect sacrifice for the sins of humanity.

5. HUMAN NAMES ARE GIVEN TO HIM BY HIMSELF AND OTHERS.

One of the ways in which we can understand the humanity of Jesus is by considering the names that are given to Him by Himself and others. In the Gospels, Jesus is referred to by various names, and many of these names emphasize His humanity.

For example, in Luke 19:10, Jesus refers to Himself as the "Son of Man." This title emphasizes His human nature, as He identifies Himself with the rest of humanity. He also refers to Himself as the "man who has authority to forgive sins" (Mark 2:10) and the "bread of life" (John 6:35).

Other names that are given to Jesus by others also emphasize His humanity. In Matthew 1:21, an angel instructs Joseph to name the child Jesus, which means "Savior." This name was a common Jewish name and emphasizes His humanity by giving Him a common name. In Acts 2:22, Peter refers to Jesus as "Jesus of Nazareth," emphasizing His earthly origin and human identity.

Moreover, Jesus is often referred to as the "Son of Man," a title that emphasizes His humanity. He uses this title over 80 times in the Gospels to refer to Himself. Even when He is referred to as the "Son of God," He sometimes immediately substitutes the title "Son of Man" (John 1:49-51; Matthew 26:63-64). By doing so, He emphasizes the reality of His human nature and His identification with humanity.

In summary, the names given to Jesus by Himself and others emphasize His humanity. The title "Son of Man" is particularly significant in this regard, as it highlights His identification with humanity and underscores His human nature. By taking on a human nature, Jesus was able to fully identify with humanity, and this enabled Him to become the perfect sacrifice for the sins of humanity.

100% GOD

1. He is Called God.

The belief that Jesus is 100% God is rooted in the idea that he possesses absolute deity. Jesus is called God in various passages of the Bible, such as John 1:1, which states that "the Word was God," indicating that Jesus is not only divine but also co-eternal and co-equal with God. Additionally, in Hebrews 1:8, God the Father refers to Jesus as "Thy throne, O God, is forever," further affirming Jesus' divine nature.

Furthermore, in John 1:18, Jesus is referred to as the "only begotten God" or "only begotten Son," further emphasizing his divinity. This is also seen in John 20:28, where the disciple Thomas addresses Jesus as "my Lord and my God," a confession of faith in Jesus' divine nature that is accepted by Christ.

Other passages, such as Romans 9:5, Titus 2:13, and 1 John 5:20, also refer to Jesus as God, clearly indicating that Jesus is not just a prophet or teacher but God himself.

2. He is Called the Son of God.

The title "Son of God" is a significant indication of Jesus' deity, and it appears numerous times throughout the Gospels. While Jesus may not have explicitly claimed this title for Himself in the synoptic Gospels, He readily accepted it when used by others to address Him. Moreover, it is clear from the charges made against Him that He was accused of claiming to be the Son of God.

In John's Gospel, Jesus unambiguously refers to Himself as the Son of God on several occasions. This Gospel begins with the statement that "the Word was God," emphasizing Jesus' divine nature from the outset. And at the end of the Gospel, Thomas' exclamation "My Lord and my God" when seeing the risen Christ provides further evidence of Jesus' deity.

In addition to being called the Son of God, Jesus is also explicitly referred to as God in several passages in the New Testament. For instance, John 1:1 describes the Word (Jesus) as God, and Hebrews 1:8 addresses Jesus as "O God." Such passages clearly affirm Jesus' divinity and indicate that He is fully God.

3. He is Called The Lord.

The term "Lord" is a significant title that is used in the Bible to refer to Jesus as God. In Acts 4:33, the apostles are said to be giving testimony to the resurrection of the Lord Jesus. In Luke 2:11, the angel announces to the shepherds that a Savior has been born to them, who is Christ the Lord. In Acts 9:17, Ananias refers to Jesus as the Lord in his conversation with Saul. These and many other passages in the Bible make it clear that the term "Lord" was a title that was reserved for God, and that it was used to refer to Jesus as God.

While it is true that the term "Lord" was used of men in certain contexts, such as when addressing a person with respect, the usage of the term for Jesus goes beyond this. In the New Testament, "Lord" is used as a title for Jesus that affirms his divine authority, power, and lordship over all creation. This title emphasizes Jesus' divine sovereignty and points to his identity as the Son of God. Therefore, Jesus is 100% God because he is called the Lord in the Bible.

4. Other Divine Names are Ascribed to Him:

In addition to the titles "God," "Son of God," and "Lord," there are other divine names ascribed to Jesus that testify to His deity. For instance, in Revelation 1:17, Jesus calls Himself "the first and the last," a title that is also used of Jehovah in several Old Testament passages (Isaiah 41:4; 44:6; 48:12). This title conveys the idea of eternal existence, implying that Jesus is not only a created being but has always existed from eternity past.

Similarly, in Revelation 22:13 and 16, Jesus identifies Himself as "the Alpha and the Omega," the first and last letters of the Greek alphabet, which again signifies His eternal nature and divinity. In Revelation 1:8, this title is used of God, emphasizing that Jesus shares the same divine nature and attributes as God the Father.

These divine names ascribed to Jesus provide further evidence of His deity, demonstrating that He is not a mere human or angelic being but is fully God. They attest to the fact that Jesus is co-eternal and co-equal with the Father, possessing all the divine attributes and prerogatives that belong to God alone.

WHY JESUS ?

1. Pre-Existence

The reason why Jesus is unique and no one else can be compared to Him is because of His pre-existence. According to the Bible, Jesus existed before He was born into the world as a human being. This is demonstrated in several passages, including John 1:1, where it says that "In the beginning was the Word, and the Word was with God, and the Word was God." This verse speaks of the eternal pre-existence of Jesus as the Word, who is identified as God.

In John 8:58, Jesus affirms His pre-existence when He says, "Before Abraham was, I am." By using the present tense "I am," Jesus is claiming to be the eternal God who existed before Abraham. This claim of pre-existence is also supported in other verses such as John 17:5, Philippians 2:6, and Colossians 1:16-17.

Therefore, Jesus is unique because He is not only fully human, but also fully God, who existed before the world began. This is what makes Him the only Savior and Redeemer of mankind, the only one who can bridge the gap between God and man and offer eternal life to those who believe in Him.

2. Self-Existence and Life-Giving Power

The self-existence and life-giving power of Jesus are significant factors in understanding why he is considered to be the only one who is 100% God. In John 5:21, Jesus claims that He has the power to give life to whomever He chooses, just as the Father has the power to raise the dead and give life. This power to give life is a clear indication of Jesus' divinity, as only God has the power to create and give life.

In John 5:26, Jesus further emphasizes his self-existence and life-giving power, saying that He has been given the same kind of life as the Father. This means that Jesus is not just a created being or a mere mortal, but rather possesses divine life that is eternal and uncreated. Similarly, John 1:4 declares that "in him was life," which means that Jesus is the source of all life and that He has the power to give life to all those who believe in him.

Hebrews 7:16 also speaks of Jesus' life-giving power, stating that He has an indestructible life that is eternal. This means that Jesus is not just a temporary being, but rather a being who has always existed and will always exist. In addition, John 17:3-5 further emphasizes Jesus' divine nature and self-existence, as Jesus claims that He existed with the Father before the world was created, and that He possesses the same glory as the Father.

Finally, in John 10:17-18, Jesus declares that He has the power to lay down his life and take it up again, which means that He has the power to overcome death and give eternal life to all those who believe in him. All of these scriptures together show that Jesus possesses self-existence and life-giving power, which are unique to God alone, and therefore is 100% God.

3. Immutability

The immutability of Jesus Christ is a crucial aspect of His deity. Immutability refers to the unchangeable and constant nature of God, which means that God does not change in His character, nature, or attributes. Jesus Christ, being God, shares in this divine attribute of immutability. In Hebrews 13:8, it states that "Jesus Christ is the same yesterday, and today, and forever." This verse assures us that Jesus remains the same and will not change.

The unchanging nature of Jesus is a source of comfort for believers, for it gives us the assurance that He will always be there for us. It is an essential aspect of our faith to know that we serve a God who is constant and steadfast, one who never changes. Moreover, Jesus Christ's immutability is an essential attribute for His redemptive work on the cross. He is the same perfect and sinless Lamb of God who offered Himself as a sacrifice for our sins.

In contrast, everything in the world is subject to change, including human teachers who come and go, but Jesus remains the same. This stability, constancy, and consistency are only found in God. Therefore, only Jesus, being God, is immutable, and this is a powerful testimony to His divine nature.

4. All the Fulness of the Godhead Dwelt in Him:

This verse in Colossians 2:9 is a powerful statement of the fullness of God dwelling in Jesus Christ. It affirms that not only did Jesus possess divine perfections and attributes, but also the very essence and nature of the Godhead. This means that Jesus is not merely a human being or a prophet, but is fully and completely God. He is the embodiment of God in human form.

This concept is central to Christian belief and is essential to understanding the unique nature of Jesus. It distinguishes Jesus from all other religious figures or leaders throughout history. No other person can claim to be fully God and fully man in the way that Jesus can.

Furthermore, this verse reveals that Jesus did not simply possess a portion of the Godhead, but rather the entirety of it. The fullness of God dwelt in Jesus, meaning that He was the perfect representation of God on earth. This is an incredible claim, but one that is fully supported by the life, teachings, and miracles of Jesus.

In short, Jesus is the only one who can be said to have the fullness of the Godhead dwelling in Him. This sets Him apart from all other religious figures and confirms His unique identity as the Son of God.

5. He is the Creator:

Jesus is worthy because He is the Creator of all things. According to John 1:3, "All things were made by Him." In other words, Jesus was the acting power and personal instrument in creation. This means that creation is a revelation of His mind and might. Hebrews 1:10 highlights the dignity of the Creator as contrasted with the creature. Colossians 1:16 contradicts the Gnostic theory of emanations and shows that Christ is the creator of all created things and beings. The phrase "the beginning of the creation of God" in Revelation 3:14 means "beginning" in the active sense, the origin, that by which a thing begins to be.

In Colossians 1:15, Jesus is referred to as the "first-born," but this does not mean that He was made. Instead, when this verse is compared with Colossians 1:17, which shows Him to be not included in the "created things," it becomes clear that He is the origin of and superior to them all. Therefore, Jesus is the Creator of the universe (Colossians 1:16) just as He is the Head of the church (Colossians 1:18). As the Creator, Jesus is worthy of our worship and adoration.

6. He is the Upholder of All Things:

The Scriptures declare that Jesus is the Upholder of all things, which means that He sustains and maintains the universe. Colossians 1:17 states, "And he is before all things, and in him all things hold together." This means that Jesus existed before all creation and that He is currently sustaining all things by His power. In Hebrews 1:3, it is stated that Jesus upholds all things by the word of His power.

This truth is significant because it reveals that Christ is not only the Creator of the universe but also its Sustainer. He is actively involved in the universe's continued existence and functioning, and without His sustaining power, everything would fall apart. This truth also demonstrates that the universe is not a closed system that operates independently of God. Instead, Christ's power actively regulates and controls the pulses of universal life.

In summary, Jesus is the Upholder of all things because He sustains and maintains the universe by His power. This truth highlights the Lord's ongoing involvement in the universe and reminds us of our dependence on Him for our very existence.

7. He Has the Right to Forgive Sins.

The fact that Jesus has the right to forgive sins is a clear indication of His divinity. In the Jewish culture, only God had the authority to forgive sins, and anyone who claimed to do so was considered a blasphemer. When Jesus forgave sins, He was claiming to possess the same divine authority as God.

In Mark 2:5-10, Jesus forgave the sins of a paralyzed man who was lowered through the roof by his friends. When the Pharisees accused Jesus of blasphemy for claiming to forgive sins, Jesus healed the man to demonstrate His authority to forgive sins. This event shows that Jesus not only had the power to forgive sins, but He also had the power to heal physical ailments, which was also considered a divine attribute.

Luke 7:48 also shows Jesus forgiving sins. A sinful woman came and anointed Jesus' feet with oil, weeping and wiping them with her hair. Jesus forgave her sins, which shocked the religious leaders who were present. This incident emphasizes that Jesus has the power to forgive any sin, regardless of how serious it may seem.

Jesus' authority to forgive sins is a clear indication that He is God. Only God can forgive sins, and when Jesus forgave sins, He was claiming to possess the same divine authority as God.

8. The Raising of the Bodies of Men is Ascribed to Him:

Jesus is the only living God because He has the power and authority to raise the dead. In the Bible, it is recorded that Jesus claimed five times that it is His prerogative to raise the dead. While others who raised the dead did so by delegated power, Jesus raised the dead by His own power. This is evident in John 10:17-18 where Jesus states that He has the power to lay down His life and to take it up again.

Not only did Jesus have the power to raise the dead, but He also claimed to have this power in the general resurrection of all men. This sets Him apart from other prophets or holy men who may have raised the dead but did not claim such power over the ultimate fate of all humanity. Jesus' ability to raise the dead was also characterized by His calmness, in contrast to the agony displayed by other prophets in performing similar miracles.

Therefore, Jesus' unique ability to raise the dead by His own power and His claim to have power over the general resurrection of all men make Him the only living God.

9. He is to be the Judge of All Men.

The Bible teaches that Jesus Christ is the judge of all men. In John 5:22, Jesus Himself declares that the Father has committed all judgment to Him. This means that Jesus has been given the authority to judge all people, both the living and the dead. This authority is not limited to a specific time or place, but extends to all of humanity throughout all of history.

This idea of Jesus as the judge of all men is reiterated in several other passages of the Bible. 2 Timothy 4:1 states that Jesus "will judge the living and the dead," while Acts 17:31 declares that God "has fixed a day on which He will judge the world in righteousness by a man whom He has appointed; and of this He has given assurance to all by raising Him from the dead." In Matthew 25:31-46, Jesus Himself gives a detailed account of the final judgment, where He separates the sheep from the goats based on how they have treated the "least of these."

The fact that Jesus will judge all men is significant because it emphasizes His sovereignty and authority over all of creation. It also underscores the seriousness of sin and the need for repentance and salvation. Those who reject Jesus as Lord and Savior will ultimately face judgment and eternal punishment, while those who receive Him will be saved and receive eternal life. As the judge of all men, Jesus is both just and merciful, and His judgment will be righteous and true.

10. Omnipotence.

Jesus is the only true living God because He is Omnipotent. This is evident in Matthew 28:18, where Jesus declares, "All power is given unto me in heaven and in earth." This means that Jesus has authority over all things in both heaven and earth. Revelation 1:8 also speaks to His omnipotence, describing Jesus as the "Alpha and the Omega, the beginning and the end...who is, and who was, and who is to come, the Almighty."

Jesus' omnipotence extends to three realms. First, He has all power on earth. He demonstrated this power during His ministry on earth, healing the sick (Luke 4:38-41), raising the dead (John

11), and even performing miracles such as turning water into wine (John 2) and calming a storm (Matthew 8).

Second, Jesus has all power in hell. He has authority over demons (Luke 4:35, 36, 41) and evil angels (Ephesians 6).

Finally, Jesus has all power in heaven. Ephesians 1:20-22 describes how God "raised Christ from the dead and seated him at his right hand in the heavenly realms, far above all rule and authority, power and dominion, and every name that is invoked, not only in the present age but also in the one to come. And God placed all things under his feet and appointed him to be head over everything for the church."

Hebrews 2:8 reinforces Jesus' omnipotence, declaring that "In putting everything under him, God left nothing that is not subject to him. Yet at present we do not see everything subject to him." And Hebrews 1:3 affirms that Jesus "is the radiance of God's glory and the exact representation of his being, sustaining all things by his powerful word."

In conclusion, Jesus' omnipotence is a powerful testimony to His deity and His unique status as the only true living God.

11. Omniscience.

Jesus is the only living God because of His omniscience, which means He has complete and perfect knowledge of all things. John 16:30 says, "Now are we sure that thou knowest all things." This verse confirms that Jesus has complete knowledge of all things. Colossians 2:3 also says, "In whom are hid all the treasures of wisdom and knowledge." Jesus is the embodiment of all wisdom and knowledge.

Throughout the Gospels, Jesus demonstrates His omniscience through His knowledge of people's thoughts and actions. In John 4:16-19, Jesus speaks with a woman at a well and tells her about her past and present circumstances, which she finds astounding. In Mark 2:8, Jesus knows what the scribes are thinking and confronts them, "Why do you question these things in your hearts?" In John 1:48, Jesus sees Nathanael before he meets Him and knows him, saying, "Before Philip called you, when you were under the fig tree, I saw you."

Jesus' omniscience also extends to knowledge of future events. In Matthew 24 and Luke 21, Jesus prophesies about the destruction of the temple and the end times. He predicts wars, earthquakes, and persecution. He also foretells His own death and resurrection.

Unlike prophets who were given knowledge through revelation, Jesus possesses immediate perception and knowledge of all things. His omniscience is not acquired but inherent. This knowledge is a divine attribute and confirms Jesus' identity as the only living God.

12. Omnipresence.

The attribute of omnipresence is often associated with God alone, as it denotes the ability to be present everywhere at the same time. In Matthew 18:20, Jesus claims this attribute for Himself, saying that wherever two or three are gathered in His name, He is present in their midst. This statement implies that Jesus is not limited by time or space, and that He can be present with multiple groups of people at the same time.

Furthermore, Jesus' promise to be with His disciples always, even to the end of the age (Matthew 28:20), indicates that His omnipresence is not limited by physical location or distance. He is able to be with His followers no matter where they are, whether they are spread out across the globe or gathered together in one place.

In 1 Corinthians 1:2, Paul addresses the church in Corinth as those who "call on the name of our Lord Jesus Christ, their Lord and ours." This suggests that the Corinthian believers were able to pray to Jesus, and that He was present to hear their prayers, no matter where they were located.

The idea of Christ's all-pervading presence is further supported by the statement in Ephesians 1:23 that Christ fills all things, every place. This means that Jesus is not limited by physical boundaries, but rather encompasses everything that exists.

Taken together, these passages suggest that Jesus possesses the attribute of omnipresence, which is traditionally associated with God alone. This is further evidence of Jesus' divine nature and reinforces the belief that He is the only living God.

13. Defeated Death

The defeat of death is a crucial aspect of Jesus' claim to be the only living God. In Colossians 2:15, it says that Jesus made a public spectacle of death and triumphed over it on the cross. This victory over death is not just a symbolic gesture; it is a tangible demonstration of Jesus' divine power.

The significance of Jesus' defeat of death cannot be overstated. Through His death and resurrection, He secured our salvation and eternal life. Romans 4:25 says that Jesus was delivered over to death for our sins and raised to life for our justification. By paying the penalty for our sins through His death, Jesus made it possible for us to be reconciled to God and receive the gift of eternal life.

Furthermore, Jesus' defeat of death is a testimony to His power and authority as the only living God. Death is the ultimate enemy of humanity, and no human being can overcome it. Yet, Jesus, as the Son of God, triumphed over death and demonstrated His divine power over all things, including life and death.

The fact that Jesus rose from the dead also validates His claims to be the Messiah and the only living God. His resurrection was witnessed by many people, including His disciples, and was recorded in the Bible. It is a historical fact that cannot be explained away by any naturalistic or humanistic explanation.

In conclusion, Jesus' defeat of death is a powerful testimony to His divine nature and authority as the only living God. Through His death and resurrection, He secured our salvation and eternal life and demonstrated His power over all things, including life and death. As believers, we can take comfort and hope in the fact that we serve a God who has overcome death and has the power to grant us eternal life.

14. Jesus Emerged the Victorious King

The passage from Philippians 2:8-11 highlights the exaltation of Jesus Christ as the victorious King. Despite being fully divine, Jesus humbled Himself by taking on human form and submitting to death on the cross, paying the ultimate price for the redemption of humanity. However, God did not leave Him in the grave, but raised Him from the dead, proving His victory over death and sin.

As a result of His obedience and sacrifice, God exalted Jesus to the highest place and gave Him the name that is above every name. Jesus is now the King of kings and Lord of lords, and every knee will bow and every tongue will confess that He is Lord. This includes not only those on earth but also those in heaven and under the earth, showing the universal authority and sovereignty of Jesus.

This exaltation of Jesus brings glory to God the Father, as it demonstrates His power and love for humanity. It also shows that Jesus is the only true living God, who has conquered death and sin, and who reigns victorious over all. As believers, we can take comfort and hope in the fact that our Savior is not only alive but is ruling and reigning in glory and power.

15. Jesus the only Way to Heaven.

The statement "Jesus is the only way to heaven" is a foundational belief of Christianity. This belief is based on Jesus' own words in John 14:6, where He declares Himself to be the way, the truth, and the life, and that no one can come to the Father except through Him. This means that only those who place their faith in Jesus Christ and accept Him as their Lord and Savior can attain eternal life in heaven.

The reason Jesus is the only path to salvation is because of His unique identity and the work He accomplished on the cross. Jesus is not just a religious leader or prophet, but He is God in human form (John 1:1-14). He came to earth to live a perfect life, die on the cross as a sacrifice for our sins, and rise again from the dead, defeating death and sin. This makes Him the only one who can reconcile us with God and provide a way to eternal life.

Other world religions may teach that salvation can be achieved through good deeds, religious rituals, or other works. However, Ephesians 2:8-9 makes it clear that salvation is a gift from God that cannot be earned through our own efforts. Only by accepting Jesus' sacrifice on the cross and putting our faith in Him can we receive salvation and eternal life.

Acts 4:12 reinforces this message, stating that there is no other name under heaven given to men by which we must be saved. This means that no other religious figure or belief system can provide salvation or lead us to heaven. Only Jesus, through His death and resurrection, has the power to save us and reconcile us with God.

Jesus is the only way to heaven because of His unique identity as God in human form, the work He accomplished on the cross, and the fact that salvation is a gift that can only be received through faith in Him. Other world religions may teach works-based salvation, but according to the Bible, only Jesus can provide eternal life.

16. No Other Name After The Name Of Jesus

The belief that Jesus is the only true living being and is worthy of praise and adoration is deeply rooted in the Christian faith. One of the reasons for this belief is the fact that there are 952 names and titles for the Trinity God, but after Jesus, no other name was given or added for God.

The concept of the Trinity in Christianity refers to the belief in one God who exists in three distinct persons - the Father, the Son (Jesus), and the Holy Spirit. Throughout the Bible, there are numerous names and titles given to God, each of which reflects a different aspect of His character and nature. These names and titles are used to describe God's power, mercy, wisdom, love, and many other attributes.

However, after the name of Jesus was given, no new names or titles for God were added. This is because Jesus is believed to be the complete and perfect revelation of God. In other words, everything that God wants us to know about Himself is revealed in the person of Jesus Christ.

The belief that Jesus is the only true living being and is worthy of praise and adoration is also based on the idea that Jesus is the only way to salvation. In John 14:6, Jesus declares, "I am the way and the truth and the life. No one comes to the Father except through me." This statement emphasizes that Jesus is the only way to God and that salvation can only be obtained through faith in Him.

Moreover, the fact that Jesus is the only way to salvation is linked to the belief that Jesus is the Son of God. The Bible tells us that Jesus is not just a prophet or a teacher, but He is the very Son of God who was sent to save humanity from sin and death. In John 3:16, it says, "For God so loved the world that he gave his one and only Son, that whoever believes in him shall not perish but have eternal life."

The name of Jesus Christ is not just a title or a mere collection of syllables. It is the name above all other names, the one name that is full of power, might, and authority. In fact, there are no other names given to God after the name of Jesus Christ, which shows the uniqueness and the importance of this name.

The Bible tells us that the name of Jesus is a name that is worthy of praise and adoration. Philippians 2:9-11 says, "Therefore God exalted him to the highest place and gave him the name that is above every name, that at the name of Jesus every knee should bow, in heaven and on earth and under the earth, and every tongue acknowledge that Jesus Christ is Lord, to the glory of God the Father."

This passage clearly emphasizes that the name of Jesus is not just any other name, but a name that has been exalted to the highest place, above all other names. This is a name that deserves to be praised and acknowledged by every living being, whether in heaven or on earth.

The uniqueness of the name of Jesus is also highlighted by the fact that there are no other names given to God after the name of Jesus Christ. Throughout the Bible, we see many different names and titles given to God, such as Jehovah, Yahweh, Elohim, Adonai, and many others. However, after the name of Jesus Christ was given, there are no new names or titles for God. This is because the name of Jesus is complete and sufficient in itself.

In fact, the Bible tells us that there is power in the name of Jesus. Acts 4:12 says, "Salvation is found in no one else, for there is no other name under heaven given to mankind by which we must be saved." This verse clearly emphasizes that salvation can only be found in the name of Jesus. It is through this name that we are able to receive forgiveness of sins and eternal life.

Furthermore, the power of the name of Jesus is not just limited to salvation. Throughout the New Testament, we see many examples of how the name of Jesus was used to perform miracles, heal the sick, and cast out demons. For example, in Acts 3:6, Peter and John heal a man who had been crippled since birth by saying, "In the name of Jesus Christ of Nazareth, walk." This miracle was performed through the power of the name of Jesus.

In conclusion, the name of Jesus Christ is not just a title or a collection of syllables. It is the name above all other names, full of power, might, and authority. There are no other names given to God after the name of Jesus Christ, which shows the uniqueness and importance of this name. It is through the name of Jesus that we are able to receive salvation and experience the power of God in our lives. Therefore, let us always praise and adore the name of Jesus Christ, for it is the name above all other names.

JESUS

- NO JESUS – NO LIFE
- KNOW JESUS – KNOW LIFE

Chapter 3

The Beginning of It All: Understanding the Story of Adam and Eve

Growing up in a cultural milieu teeming with diverse narratives of creation, the story of Adam and Eve, as depicted in the Bible, became a pivotal anchor in my quest for understanding our origin and connection with the divine. It wasn't just a historical account but a profound revelation of our shared heritage.

According to the sacred scriptures, God intricately crafted Adam and Eve, marking the inception of humanity—a lineage I am undeniably part of. The notion that we, as their descendants, bear the indelible image of God resonated with me on a personal level. It transcended biology, delving into the very core of our existence, shaping our morality, spirituality, and intellect.

In this chapter, I extend an invitation to journey alongside me into the sacred narrative of Adam. It's more than a theological exploration; it's an intimate quest to fathom the depths of our identity as human beings created in the very image of God. As we traverse the unfolding story of Adam, we'll unravel the threads that weave our purpose and destiny into the grand tapestry of creation.

The concept of being created in God's image isn't a mere theological abstraction; it's a profound reality that shapes the contours of our existence. Through the lens of Adam's story, we'll peer into the significance of this divine imprint on our humanity and how it intricately ties into our purpose and destiny. Yet, the narrative doesn't end in pristine perfection.

We'll confront the stark reality of the fall—the unraveling of our harmonious relationship with God and its enduring repercussions on our interactions today. The echoes of Adam's choices reverberate through generations, underscoring the desperate need for redemption and restoration—a need that finds its fulfillment in the transformative power of Christ.

This isn't just a chapter in the annals of ancient history; it's a mirror reflecting the intricacies of our identity, echoing the timeless call for redemption. As we journey through the story of Adam, my hope is that you, too, will discover, with fresh eyes, the profound implications of our shared heritage and the transformative power of redemption through Christ.

This narrative isn't a mere alternative to evolutionary theories; it's a transcendent truth that elevates the preciousness of our lives. Unlike a narrative that places us as descendants of animals, it asserts that we are fearfully and wonderfully made, bearing the very image of God. This revelation imparts a profound sense of dignity and purpose, emphasizing that our existence is not a product of chance but a deliberate act of divine craftsmanship.

The word "adam" is a Hebrew term that has several meanings in the Bible. It can be used as a noun to refer to a human being, both individually and collectively. When used collectively, it refers to all of humanity, as seen in Genesis 1:27, which says, "So God created man (adam) in his own image, in the image of God he created him; male and female he created them." Here, the word "adam" is used to describe the entirety of the human race.

When used individually, "adam" can refer to a specific human being, as seen in Genesis 2:7, which says, "Then the Lord God formed a man (adam) from the dust of the ground and breathed into his nostrils the breath of life, and the man (adam) became a living being." In this verse, the word "adam" refers to the first human being, whom God created from the dust of the earth and breathed life into.

It's worth noting that the word "adam" is gender nonspecific and can refer to both men and women. This is seen in Genesis 5:1-2, which says, "When God created man (adam), he made him in the likeness of God. Male and female he created them, and he blessed them and named them Man (adam) when they were created." Here, "adam" is used to refer to both men and women, emphasizing the equality of both genders in God's eyes.

Lastly, the word "adam" can also be used specifically to refer to a male human being, as seen in Genesis 2:23-24, which says, "The man (adam) said, 'This is now bone of my bones and flesh of my flesh; she shall be called 'woman,' for she was taken out of man (adam).' For this reason, a man (adam) will leave his father and mother and be united to his wife, and they will become one flesh." Here, "adam" refers specifically to the first man, who named his wife "woman" because she was taken out of him.

In summary, the word "adam" has multiple meanings in the Bible and can refer to humanity as a whole, a specific individual, or a male human being.

Eve

- Eve was God's last creation and was created to be Adam's companion.

- According to the Bible, Eve was created from one of Adam's ribs while he was in a deep sleep. This act symbolizes the unity and partnership between man and woman in marriage.

- God created Eve to be Adam's "helper", which is sometimes interpreted as a subordinate role, but in reality refers to a complementary partnership where both the man and the woman work together to fulfill God's purposes.

- The creation of Eve highlights the importance of relationships and companionship in the human experience. God recognized that it was not good for Adam to be alone and so He created Eve to be his partner and helper.

- The story of Eve's creation also shows God's intention for marriage to be a sacred and lifelong commitment between a man and a woman, united in love and partnership.

- The name "Eve" means "life" or "living", and reflects the vital role that women play in bringing new life into the world through childbirth.

- The creation of Eve is an example of God's love and care for humanity, and His desire for us to experience deep and meaningful relationships with one another.

God's Own Image

The concept that humans are created in the image of God is a central belief in Christianity. It means that humans are not just physical beings, but they also possess moral, spiritual, and intellectual qualities that reflect God's nature. This belief is rooted in the Biblical account of creation in Genesis 1:27, which states, "So God created mankind in his own image, in the image of God he created them; male and female he created them."

It is important to note that the phrase "in God's image" does not refer to physical appearance, but rather to the essence of what it means to be human. This includes our ability to reason, our capacity for moral judgment, our ability to create, and our capacity for relationships.

In Genesis 2:7, we see that God created Adam from the dust of the ground and breathed into him the breath of life, making him a living being. This demonstrates that there is something unique about human beings, something that sets us apart from the rest of creation.

Similarly, when God created Eve, he did so by taking a rib from Adam's side, symbolizing that they were to be companions and equal partners in life. This shows that the image of God is not limited to one gender or the other, but is shared equally by both men and women.

Overall, the concept of humans being created in God's image speaks to the inherent value and dignity of every person, regardless of race, gender, or any other characteristic. It also emphasizes our responsibility to reflect God's nature and character in our thoughts, actions, and relationships.

God's Best Work

The concept of being God's best work is rooted in the belief that we were intentionally created by God with a purpose and a plan. Psalm 139:13-14 describes how God intricately designed us and knitted us together in our mother's womb, and we are fearfully and wonderfully made. This means that we are unique and have inherent value simply because we were created by God.

Ephesians 2:10 also reinforces this idea by stating that we are God's masterpiece, created anew in Christ Jesus for good works that God has already prepared for us. This means that we were created with a specific purpose and that God has equipped us with the necessary abilities and gifts to fulfill that purpose.

Understanding that we are God's best work can help us develop a positive self-image and recognize the worth and value of others as well. It reminds us that we are not here by accident but by design, and we have a meaningful role to play in God's plan.

The idea that humankind is the best creation of God is a reflection of the unique attributes and qualities that humans possess. Unlike the rest of creation, humans were created in God's own image and given a special role to play in His plan. This role includes the ability to have a relationship with God, to use our free will to make choices, to be stewards of the earth, and to bring glory to God through our actions.

The Bible affirms this idea in several passages. For instance, in Psalm 8:4-6, the psalmist writes, "what is mankind that you are mindful of them, human beings that you care for them? You have made them a little lower than the angels and crowned them with glory and honor. You made them rulers over the works of your hands; you put everything under their feet." This passage highlights the unique position that humans hold in the hierarchy of creation.

Additionally, in Ephesians 2:10, Paul writes that "we are God's masterpiece, created anew in Christ Jesus." This verse affirms that we are not just another creature in God's creation, but rather we are His best work. We were created to be unique and special, with a purpose that only we can fulfill.

Therefore, as humans, we should recognize and embrace our unique position in God's creation. We should strive to live in a way that brings glory to God and fulfills our purpose on earth. We should also be grateful for the gifts and abilities that God has given us, and use them to serve others and make a positive impact in the world.

But Why ?

1. We were created to serve and keep: According to Genesis 2:15, God created human beings to serve and keep the Earth. This implies that we have a responsibility to care for the planet and its resources, and to use them in a responsible manner.

2. To be fruitful and multiply: In Genesis 1:28, God commands Adam and Eve to be fruitful and multiply. This indicates that procreation is an essential part of our purpose and that we should strive to create and nurture life.

3. We were created to be with God: Genesis 3:8 shows that human beings were created to have a close relationship with God. This implies that our ultimate goal should be to seek and maintain this relationship, and that we should prioritize our spiritual lives.

4. We were created to listen to God: Genesis 2:16-17 shows that obedience to God's commands is an essential part of our purpose. This means that we should strive to understand and follow God's will, as revealed through scripture and prayer.

5. We were created to act like God: Genesis 1:28 and Romans 12:2 suggest that we were created to act like God, reflecting His nature and values in our actions and attitudes. This implies that we should strive to live a life of love, kindness, and compassion towards others.

6. Worship His Name: According to Isaiah 43:21, we were created to worship God's name. This means that we should honor

and glorify God in our daily lives, through prayer, worship, and acts of service.

7. God created us to live and enjoy relationship as He did: John 15:11 suggests that our purpose is to experience the joy of living in close relationship with God. This means that we should prioritize our spiritual lives, seeking to cultivate a close relationship with God and experiencing the joy and fulfillment that comes from this relationship.

Overall, the Bible suggests that our purpose as human beings is to serve and care for the Earth, procreate, seek and maintain a close relationship with God, listen to His commands, act like Him, worship His name, and experience the joy of living in close relationship with Him. By fulfilling these purposes, we can reflect God's presence and give Him glory.

Chapter 4

The Dilemma of Disobedience: Delving into the Concept of Sin

Sin, like a pervasive and corrosive force, weaves its way through the fabric of our world, leaving in its wake a trail of pain and suffering. Its insidious presence touches every aspect of our lives, creating a chasm that separates us from the very source of goodness and life—God. In this chapter, I invite you to join me on a personal exploration of sin, a journey into its depths, understanding its multifaceted nature, and unraveling its impact on our existence.

Sin, for me, is not an abstract concept but a stark reality that manifests in various forms—sins of commission and sins of omission. It's the harsh words spoken in anger, the moments of selfishness that stain the canvas of our lives, and the opportunities to do good left untouched. It's a force that blinds us to the beauty of God's intended life for us.

As we embark on this exploration, we'll confront the devastating consequences of sin—the spiritual death that creeps into our souls, poisoning the well of our relationship with God. It's a separation, a darkness that threatens to engulf us. But fear not, for woven into the narrative of sin is the thread of redemption, the promise of overcoming through the transformative power of the Holy Spirit.

In sharing this journey, my aim is not to dwell solely on the shadows but to illuminate the path toward the grace and mercy offered by God through Jesus Christ. Understanding the nature of sin becomes a compass guiding us toward the shores of redemption. It's an acknowledgment of our frailties met with the overwhelming love of a God who extends His hand to lift us from the depths.

As we delve into the intricacies of sin, may we not be disheartened but inspired to live in a way that honors the One who offers redemption. Through our understanding of sin's grip, we unearth a deeper appreciation for the grace that covers our shortcomings. Let us strive to walk in the light of this knowledge, bringing joy not only to ourselves but radiating it to those we encounter on this journey called life.

During my years pursuing a Bachelor's degree in Theology in the vibrant city of Kolkata from 2008 to 2011, a particular incident stands out in my memory—an encounter that etched into my heart the stark reality of the world's need for redemption. In those formative years, I took to the bustling student food street near my college to share the transformative message of the Gospel.

As I engaged with the diverse crowd, I encountered a young woman who became emblematic of the challenges in conveying the profound message of repentance and salvation. In the midst of the aromatic street food and lively chatter, I approached her with the earnestness that comes from a deep conviction in the life-changing power of Jesus Christ.

Our dialogue swiftly transformed into a heated exchange as I, driven by my faith, emphasized the need for repentance from a lifestyle contrary to biblical principles. In particular, I addressed the topic of sexual sins and the call to purity, urging her to reconsider her choices. Little did I anticipate the raw honesty that would follow.

In a moment of startling candor, she candidly shared that, for her, engaging in intimate relationships with multiple partners before marriage was merely a form of recreation—an exercise, as she put it, that rejuvenated her spirit. The clash of perspectives was evident, highlighting the profound gap between the biblical worldview and the cultural norms embraced by many.

This encounter was a poignant reminder that the message of salvation often faces resistance when challenging societal norms. Yet, it also reinforced the urgency of the mission to bring the light of Christ to places overshadowed by worldly values. As an individual committed to sharing the Gospel, these moments of tension serve as a driving force to continue spreading the message of hope, even in the face of disagreement and cultural divergence. Through these encounters, the reality of sin becomes not just a theological concept but a palpable force, underscoring the desperate need for the transformative power of Christ's love.

1. Sin is disobedience to God: The Bible defines sin as a violation of God's commands or instructions. It is fundamentally a rebellion against God's authority and His will for our lives. The story of Adam and Eve in Genesis 3 illustrates the concept of sin as disobedience to God's commands. The serpent tempted Eve to eat from the forbidden tree, and she and Adam both chose to disobey God's instructions. This act of disobedience introduced sin into the world and separated humanity from God.

2. God's rules for human life: According to the Bible, God has laid down rules and guidelines for human beings to live in a way

that is pleasing to Him and brings fulfilment and happiness. These rules are revealed in scripture and include commands to love God and love others, to live with integrity and honesty, and to avoid behaviours that are harmful to ourselves or others.

3. Sin as rebellion against God: When we choose to disobey God's commands or act in ways that are contrary to His will, we are engaging in rebellion against God's authority. This separates us from Him and damages our relationship with Him.

4. Romans 2:14-15: These verses suggest that even those who do not have access to the written law are held accountable for their actions. The moral law is written on the hearts of all human beings, and we are expected to live in accordance with this law, whether or not we have access to the written scriptures.

Sin is fundamentally a disobedience to God and His commands, and it separates us from Him and damages our relationship with Him. By living in accordance with God's rules and seeking forgiveness for our sins, we can strive to restore our relationship with Him and live a life that is pleasing to Him.

In the Old Testament, there are several Hebrew words used to describe sin and its various aspects. Dr. Charles Ryrie has identified at least eight basic Hebrew words used to describe sin:

1. Ra: This word means "bad" and is used to describe actions that are morally wrong or evil. For example, in Genesis 38:7, Judah's actions with Tamar are described as "evil" or "bad."

2. Rasha: This word means "wickedness" and is used to describe those who are actively and intentionally doing wrong. In Exodus 2:13, we see the Egyptians acting wickedly towards the Israelites.

3. Asham: This word means "guilt" and is used to describe the feeling of remorse or regret that comes from knowing that one has done something wrong. In Hosea 4:15, Israel is described as feeling guilty for their idolatry.

4. Chata: This word means "sin" and is one of the most commonly used words to describe wrongdoing. In Exodus 20:20, Moses tells the Israelites not to be afraid of God when He speaks, but to "not sin" by disobeying His commands.

5. Avon: This word means "iniquity" and refers to actions that are twisted or crooked, often implying a deliberate attempt to deceive or mislead. In 1 Samuel 3:13, Eli's sons are described as committing "iniquity" by taking the choicest portions of the sacrifices for themselves.

6. Shagag: This word means "err" or "wander" and refers to actions that are unintentionally wrong or mistaken. In Isaiah 28:7, the priests and prophets are described as being drunk and wandering in their vision, leading them to make errors in judgment.

7. Taah: This word means "wander away" or "go astray" and is often used to describe the act of turning away from God's commands. In Ezekiel 48:11, the people of Israel are described as having "gone astray" from God's laws.

8. Pasha: This word means "rebel" or "transgress" and is used to describe actions that are actively and intentionally going against God's commands. In 1 Kings 8:50, Solomon prays for forgiveness for the people of Israel when they "transgress" against God.

These various words used in the Hebrew language to describe sin highlight the different aspects and nuances of wrongdoing, from unintentional mistakes to intentional rebellion against God.

Here's a brief explanation of each of the twelve words used to describe sin in the New Testament:

1. Kakos: This word is often translated as "bad" and can refer to anything that is morally or ethically wrong. In Romans 13:3, it is used to describe those who do evil and should be afraid of punishment.

2. Poneros: This word means "evil" and can refer to anything that is wicked or harmful. In Matthew 5:45, Jesus speaks of how God causes the sun to rise on both the good and the evil, suggesting that even those who do evil are still under God's care.

3. Asebes: This word means "godless" and can refer to those who do not acknowledge God or who reject His authority. In Romans 1:18, Paul writes about how God's wrath is revealed against those who suppress the truth in unrighteousness.

4. Enochos: This word means "guilt" and can refer to the state of being responsible for wrongdoing. In Matthew 5:21, Jesus warns that anyone who is angry with his brother is liable to judgment.

5. Hamartia: This is the most common word for "sin" in the New Testament and can refer to any action or thought that falls short of God's perfect standard. In 1 Corinthians 6:18, Paul writes about how sexual immorality is a sin against one's own body.

6. Adikia: This word means "unrighteousness" and can refer to any action that violates God's law or standard of justice. In 1 Corinthians 6:9, Paul warns that the unrighteous will not inherit the kingdom of God.

7. Anomos: This word means "lawlessness" and can refer to any action that is contrary to God's law or order. In 1 Timothy 1:9,

Paul writes about how the law is not made for the righteous, but for the lawless and disobedient.

8. Parabates: This word means "transgression" and can refer to any action that goes beyond the limits set by God's law. In Romans 5:14, Paul writes about how sin was in the world before the law, but transgression is not counted where there is no law.

9. Agnoein: This word means "to be ignorant" and can refer to any lack of knowledge or understanding. In Romans 1:13, Paul writes about how he wanted to come to Rome to preach the gospel, but had been prevented from doing so.

10. Planan: This word means "to go astray" and can refer to any action that leads one away from God's truth or righteousness. In 1 Corinthians 6:9, Paul warns that those who engage in homosexuality or adultery will not inherit the kingdom of God.

11. Paraptomai: This word means "to fall away" and can refer to any action that leads one to abandon or reject God's truth or righteousness. In Galatians 6:1, Paul encourages those who have fallen away to restore them gently, so as not to fall into temptation themselves.

12. Hupocrites: This word means "hypocrite" and can refer to anyone who pretends to be something they are not. In 1 Timothy 4:2, Paul warns about those who will abandon the faith and follow deceitful spirits and teachings of demons.

The Fall

The concept of the fall and sin refers to the moment in the biblical narrative when Adam and Eve disobeyed God's command not to eat from the Tree of the Knowledge of Good and Evil. This act is considered a turning point in the relationship between humanity and God. Prior to this event, God had created a good universe and good human beings, but the disobedience of Adam and Eve led to a fundamental shift in the nature of humanity and its relationship with God.

In the biblical account of the fall, the Tempter approaches Eve and calls into question God's truthfulness, sovereignty, and goodness. The Tempter uses cunning tactics to deflect the woman's attention from the covenantal relationship God had established with humanity. He convinces her to doubt God's word and to take matters into her own hands. This temptation ultimately leads to the fall of humanity.

The fatal sequence of events that follows unfolds rapidly. Eve "saw" that the fruit of the tree was good for food and pleasing to the eye, and she "took" some and "ate" it. She then "gave" some to Adam, who also ate it. This act of disobedience had far-reaching consequences for humanity. It resulted in the loss of the original relationship between humanity and God and introduced sin into the world.

Sin separates humanity from God, and it can lead to spiritual death. However, the Bible also provides a path to redemption through the sacrifice of Jesus Christ. Through faith in Christ, humans can be reconciled with God and find freedom from the power of sin.

After eating the fruit, Adam and Eve experience a drastic change in their emotions and relationships. They immediately feel shame and realize their nakedness, which was previously unproblematic. Their eyes are now opened to the reality of their sin and the resulting separation from God. In their attempt to hide from God, they reveal their fear and estrangement from Him.

The consequences of their disobedience extend beyond their relationship with God. They also experience dissonance in their relationship with each other. Eve blames the serpent for deceiving her, and Adam blames both Eve and God for giving her to him as a companion. Their unity is now broken, and they experience a sense of isolation from each other.

The punishment for their disobedience is also severe. God tells the woman that she will experience pain in childbirth, and the man will have to toil to cultivate the ground, which will yield thorns and thistles. These physical hardships reflect the spiritual pain that sin brings into their lives.

The fall of Adam and Eve has significant implications for all humanity. It introduces sin and death into the world and separates us from God. It demonstrates the destructive power of disobedience and the need for redemption. However, it also reveals God's grace and mercy as He provides a way for us to be reconciled to Him through faith in Jesus Christ.

1. Sin is always presented in an appealing and attractive package that can deceive people. The temptation to sin can be so strong that people often overlook the consequences and fail to consider the long-term effects of their actions. In the Bible, the account of Adam and Eve in Genesis 3 shows how sin can be disguised in a beautiful package. Eve saw that the tree was beautiful and its fruit looked delicious, and she was convinced to take some and eat it. Sin often appears to be harmless and beneficial in the short term, but its ultimate consequences can be devastating.

2. Sin is always targeted and personalized. The devil targeted Jesus in the wilderness, and he tempts each of us in our areas of weakness. In Matthew 4:1-11, the devil offers Jesus various things

that would appeal to him, such as bread when he was hungry and power when he was weak. Sin can be tailor-made to suit an individual's desires, and it often manifests itself in specific areas of life that are vulnerable to attack.

3. Sin often begins with small steps. David's sin with Bathsheba in 2 Samuel 11 illustrates how a small action can lead to a big problem. David's initial sin was only to look at Bathsheba, but this led to a chain reaction of events that ultimately resulted in adultery, deceit, and murder. Sin often starts with small actions, which can quickly escalate into larger and more serious sins.

Sin is always packaged attractively, targeted personally, and often begins with small steps. It is important to be vigilant and aware of these tactics of sin, and to resist its temptations by relying on God's strength and guidance.

The consequences of sin are severe and far-reaching, affecting both our temporal and eternal lives. In the Bible, Romans 6:23 states that "the wages of sin is death," which implies that sin has a payment and the payment is death. This refers not only to physical death, but also to eternal separation from God. Sin separates us from God, creating a divide between us and Him that is insurmountable without divine intervention.

1. Death: Sin leads to physical death, which is a direct result of the fall of humanity. When Adam and Eve sinned, death became a reality for all people (Romans 5:12). This physical death is a reminder of the spiritual death that we experience as a result of sin, which is eternal separation from God (Revelation 20:14-15).

2. Separation from God: Sin creates a barrier between us and God. Isaiah 59:2 says, "But your iniquities have separated you from your God; your sins have hidden his face from you, so that

he will not hear." When we sin, we turn away from God and choose to follow our own desires. This separation from God is devastating because it prevents us from experiencing the love, joy, and peace that comes from being in a relationship with Him.

3. Brokenness in relationships: Sin not only creates a separation between us and God, but it also creates brokenness in our relationships with others. Sin causes us to act selfishly and hurt others, which can damage relationships and create bitterness and resentment. This brokenness can be seen in all aspects of our lives, including our families, friendships, and even society as a whole.

4. Guilt and shame: Sin produces guilt and shame, which can weigh heavily on us and prevent us from experiencing true freedom and joy. When we sin, we know that we have done something wrong, and this can lead to feelings of guilt and shame. However, God offers forgiveness and restoration through Jesus Christ, who paid the price for our sins on the cross. When we confess our sins and turn to Him, we can experience freedom from guilt and shame and receive the gift of eternal life.

The Ultimate solution to sin through Jesus:

• The problem of sin is a fundamental issue that affects every human being, as all have sinned and fall short of the glory of God (Romans 3:23). Sin separates us from God and leads to eternal death, both physically and spiritually (Romans 6:23).

• The Old Testament law prescribed animal sacrifices to atone for sin, as God declared that without the shedding of blood there is no forgiveness of sins (Hebrews 9:22). These sacrifices were a temporary solution, pointing forward to the ultimate sacrifice of Jesus Christ.

- Jesus is the ultimate solution to sin because he offered himself as the perfect, once-for-all sacrifice for sin. He is the Lamb of God who takes away the sin of the world (John 1:29). His blood was shed on the cross to provide forgiveness for sins (Ephesians 1:7).

- Through faith in Jesus Christ, we can receive forgiveness for our sins and be reconciled to God. Jesus said, "I am the way, the truth, and the life. No one comes to the Father except through me" (John 14:6).

- The death of Jesus was not the end, as he rose from the dead on the third day, demonstrating his power over sin and death. Through his resurrection, he offers eternal life to all who believe in him (Romans 6:5).

- The sacrifice of Jesus was an act of love, as he willingly laid down his life for his friends (John 15:13). This love is the ultimate expression of God's grace and mercy towards us, as he offers salvation to all who believe in Jesus Christ (Ephesians 2:8-9).

In summary, the solution to sin is found in Jesus Christ, who offered himself as the perfect sacrifice for sin and rose from the dead to offer eternal life to all who believe in him. Through faith in Jesus, we can receive forgiveness for our sins and be reconciled to God, experiencing the fullness of his grace and mercy.

• OUR RESPONSE TO SIN

1. Repent (1 John 1:9) - Acknowledge your wrongdoing and turn away from it. Ask God for forgiveness and cleansing. Confessing our sins to God and asking for forgiveness is an important step in seeking restoration in our relationship with Him.

2. Go and Sin No More (John 8:11) - Once we have repented, we should make a conscious effort to turn away from sin and avoid

situations that might lead us into temptation. We should strive to live a life that is pleasing to God and aligned with His will.

3. Renew a Right Spirit Psalms 51:7-11 - nlt

• David's psalm of repentance serves as an example of how we can respond to sin. We can ask God to purify us from our sins, restore our joy, remove the stain of guilt, create in us a clean heart, and renew a loyal spirit within us. This means allowing God to transform us from the inside out, changing our hearts and our desires to align with His will.

4. Seek accountability - It can be helpful to have trusted friends or mentors who can hold us accountable in our efforts to turn away from sin and live a righteous life. They can offer support, encouragement, and guidance as we navigate the challenges of life.

5. Trust in God's grace - While it is important to take responsibility for our actions and seek to live a righteous life, we must also remember that we are not saved by our own efforts. Salvation comes through faith in Jesus Christ and the grace of God. We should trust in God's forgiveness and mercy, knowing that He is always willing to forgive us and help us grow in our relationship with Him.

Chapter 5

From Sin to Salvation: Embracing the Path to Redemption

I was born and brought up in a Christian family, I am a third generation Christian in my family. My grandfather was the first Christian in his family, he was given a choice to choose between Jesus or his property but he proudly choose Jesus for him and his family, because of the choice he had to lose all his inheritance that you would have got from his family. I still remember when my father's elder brother(Rev. Sisira Kanta Dip) was alive he was sitting with me one day and was telling me the stories of how it was for them to come to Christ, the story goes like this that there was a census is going on in our area and the people who came to do the census ask my grandfather that what is religion is that they can put on the paper for the government many people in that area wrote Gonda-Christian meaning scheduled caste Christian means that they are believers but they don't want to lose the privilege of being a schedule cast which the government gives to the schedule caste and not to the general people because if someone becomes a Christian legally then he or she will lose all the benefits that the government gives for a schedule caste or a scheduled tribe person in India, rather he told the guy to write CHRISTIAN in the religion column in block letters because he was proud of his decision of following Jesus that's the story of salvation of my family. My father had his own testimony like that and likewise I have my own testimony and story of how I became a Christian or how I started following Jesus as my Lord and saviour, salvation is a very personal think it cannot be a generational thing that because my grandfather was such a radical believer that he left everything because of Jesus that won't be the same case for me or for someone else salvation is a personal experience that everyone has to experience to have Jesus as their Lord and Saviour in their lives. As I shared the story of my grandfather who did everything he could in his time doesn't guarantee me my salvation because of his faithfulness I am not getting salvation and that's the truth. Salvation has to be a personal encounter with Jesus and accepting him as the Lord and saviour in my personal life, not for my family not for me Church not for anyone else salvation is personal because your saviour is personal. That's where I received Jesus as my Lord and saviour in the year 2004 and got baptised in the year 2005 November 25th and started my journey with my Lord and Saviour and 2007 the Lord help me to start my own Ministries to save people specially young people in India because before accepting Jesus is my Lord and saviour I was not living a life that was not right. Even though I was born in a Christian family by the time I was in my teenage I started using different kinds of intoxicating things to please myself I started living my life with friends who were into drugs and all the other things my life was not right at all, I have done so many things that people can't even imagine. As a young man I was lost in the world even though my father was a pastor my life was not even close to a Christian life. I was a disgrace to my family and to my church, no one would like to associate themselves with my name or with me in anyways. That was the time when I was left all alone only with few friends who just wanted me to become like them and get lost in the in the worldly pleasures, not to be surprised some of my old friends have already died because of the heavy use of drugs and alcohol. Then I found out that there is nobody else who can love me as Jesus loves me and one fine day I decided to follow Jesus in 2004 and after that I have never looked back and I can tell you this that that decision is the best decision I have ever taken in my life. In 2007 the Lord gave me the vision to start the Ministry called Life For Christ Ministry because I give my life for so many people and so many things but from now onwards I wanted to give my life only for rest so I called my Ministries the Life For Christ Ministries. The vision statement was very simple saving souls for eternity and that's what I am still doing and by the end of 2023 now my ministry has impacted more than 500,000 lives in India and in neighbouring countries and now even in Africa. My vision is clear "Saving Souls for Eternity".

Salvation is a cornerstone of the Christian faith, representing the ultimate expression God's love and grace towards humanity. It is the process by which individuals are saved from the bondage of sin and reconciled with God, allowing them to enjoy an abundant life on earth and an eternal life in heaven. The importance of salvation in the Christian life cannot be overstated, as it forms the foundation of our relationship with God and our purpose for existence. Through salvation, we receive forgiveness, hope, peace, and a new identity in Christ, transforming our lives and enabling us to fulfill our God-given destiny.

Salvation is a central concept in Christianity, and it carries a significant meaning for Christians around the world. The term "salvation" can be defined as the process of being rescued from the consequences of sin, which separates us from God. This idea of being saved is not limited to Christianity alone, as many other religious traditions also hold similar beliefs. However, in Christianity, salvation holds a much deeper meaning.

Salvation is not merely an escape from eternal punishment, but it also involves a process of being reconciled with God and being transformed by the Holy Spirit. Through salvation, Christians believe that they can have a personal relationship with God and experience His grace and love. The Bible teaches that salvation is available to all people, regardless of their past or present circumstances.

The concept of salvation is described in various terms in the Bible, including Mukti, Moksha, Nijat, Udhhar, and Paritarn. These terms emphasize the idea of being freed or released from something, whether it be bondage, suffering, or sin. Christians believe that salvation is made possible through the life, death, and resurrection of Jesus Christ, who paid the price for our sins and opened the way for us to be reconciled with God.

Salvation is not a one-time event, but rather an ongoing process of growth and transformation. As Christians, we are called to continue to grow in our faith and pursue a life of righteousness, as we await the ultimate fulfillment of our salvation in the Kingdom of God. In summary, salvation is an essential part of the Christian life, offering a way to be reconciled with God and experience His love and grace.

The concept of salvation is deeply rooted in the Bible and is fundamental to the Christian faith. The word "salvation" is derived from the Greek word "soteria" and the Hebrew word "yasha," which both convey the idea of being rescued, delivered, or freed. In essence, salvation refers to the process by which a person is saved from sin and its consequences, and is reconciled to God.

The concept of salvation implies that there is something from which one needs to be saved. According to the Bible, all human beings are born with a sinful nature and are separated from God as a result. The consequences of sin include death, both physical and spiritual. However, God has made a way for humanity to be saved from sin and its consequences through Jesus Christ.

In Christianity, salvation is seen as a gift from God that cannot be earned through human effort or good works. Rather, it is a result of faith in Jesus Christ as Lord and Savior. This faith involves a repentance of sins and a commitment to follow Jesus Christ.

Salvation, therefore, is not merely about escaping hell or eternal punishment. It is about being reconciled to God, experiencing a transformed life, and ultimately, eternal life with God. The Bible teaches that salvation is available to all who believe in Jesus Christ and put their faith in Him.

THE DOCTRINE OF SALVATION

1. CONDEMNATION: The Desperate NEED for Salvation This refers to the idea that all human beings are born into a state of sin, due to the disobedience of Adam and Eve in the Garden of Eden. As a result, we are all separated from God and deserve eternal punishment. The only way to escape this condemnation is through faith in Jesus Christ, who paid the penalty for our sins on the cross.

2. ELECTION: The Eternal PLAN for Salvation This refers to the idea that salvation is not something we earn or achieve on our own, but rather is a gift of God's grace. It is the result of God's eternal plan, and not something we could have accomplished through our own efforts.

3. REDEMPTION: The Gracious PROVISION for Salvation This refers to the idea that Jesus Christ, through His death and resurrection, has paid the price for our sins and provided a way for us to be reconciled to God. Through faith in Him, we are redeemed from the penalty of our sins.

4. JUSTIFICATION: The Personal IMPUTATION of Salvation This refers to the idea that when we place our faith in Jesus Christ, we are not only forgiven of our sins, but also credited with His righteousness. This is known as imputed righteousness, and it means that when God looks at us, He sees the perfect righteousness of Christ.

5. REGENERATION: The Immediate BLESSINGS of Salvation This refers to the idea that when we place our faith in Jesus Christ, we are born again spiritually. This is a work of the Holy Spirit, who indwells us and begins to transform us from the inside out.

6. SANCTIFICATION: The Resultant FRUITS of Salvation This refers to the ongoing process of transformation that occurs in the life of a believer. As we grow in our relationship with God, we are gradually conformed to the image of Christ, and the fruits of the Spirit (love, joy, peace, patience, etc.) become increasingly evident in our lives.

7. PRESERVATION: The Eternal SECURITY of Salvation This refers to the idea that once we are saved, we are always saved. This is not based on our own ability to keep ourselves saved, but rather on the fact that our salvation is secured by the power of God. As Jesus said, "My sheep listen to my voice; I know them, and they follow me. I give them eternal life, and they

shall never perish; no one will snatch them out of my hand" (John 10:27-28).

8. GLORIFICATION: The Future GLORY of Salvation
This refers to the ultimate goal of our salvation, which is to be glorified with Christ in heaven. When we die or when Christ returns, our bodies will be raised and transformed, and we will be with Him forever in a state of perfect joy and peace.

WHAT ARE WE SAVED FROM ?

The salvation that is important to God is the salvation from sin and its consequences.

1. The New Testament word for salvation sometimes refers to deliverance from physical threats, but the main focus is on deliverance from the consequences of sin, including the power of death and Satan.

2. The major theme of deliverance in the New Testament is the deliverance from God's wrath.

3. In 1 Thessalonians 1:10, the apostle Paul writes that Jesus delivers us from the coming wrath of God.

4. Romans 5:9 also speaks of our being delivered from the wrath to come through Jesus Christ.

5. The wrath of God is a common theme in the Bible and is the righteous judgment and punishment of God against sin and evil.

6. In order to be saved from God's wrath, we must turn away from sin and put our faith in Jesus Christ as our Lord and Savior.

7. Through his sacrifice on the cross, Jesus has made a way for us to be saved from sin, death, and the wrath of God.

8. Salvation is not just about avoiding punishment, but it is about being reconciled to God and living in a right relationship with Him.

As Christians, we are called to live a life that reflects our gratitude for the salvation we have received and to share the good news of salvation with others.

BY WHOM ARE WE SAVED ?

1. The Philippian jailer's question - In Acts 16:30, a jailer asked Paul and Silas, "Sirs, what must I do to be saved?" This question demonstrates that salvation is a universal concern for all people, regardless of social status or background.

2. Jesus as the only means of salvation - In response to the jailer's question, Paul and Silas pointed him to Jesus Christ as the only means by which a person can be saved. This points to the exclusivity of the Christian faith in terms of salvation.

3. God enacts salvation - While we are responsible for responding to God's call to salvation, ultimately it is God who enacts salvation in our lives. We cannot save ourselves through good works or any other means.

4. Trusting in God - Psalm 20 emphasizes the importance of trusting in God for salvation, rather than relying on material possessions or other people.

5. Jesus came to save sinners - 1 Timothy 1:15 emphasizes the universality of salvation, stating that Jesus came to save sinners of all backgrounds and walks of life.

Overall, these points emphasize that salvation is a universal concern for all people, that Jesus is the only means of salvation, and that God is the one who enacts salvation in our lives. It also stresses the importance of trusting in God for salvation and acknowledging our own sinfulness.

Christ Became The Sinners Substitute So That We Would:

1. Have life (Jn. 6:51): Jesus Christ, as the Savior of the world, gave His life on the cross to provide eternal life to those who believe in Him. Through His death and resurrection, He conquered sin and death, and offers us the gift of everlasting life.

2. Be made righteous (II Cor. 5:21): As sinners, we are unable to make ourselves righteous in the eyes of God. But Jesus Christ, by taking our sins upon Himself on the cross, has made it possible for us to be counted as righteous before God.

3. Be delivered from this present evil world (Gal. 1:4): The world we live in is full of sin and corruption. But through faith in Christ, we can be delivered from the power of sin and live as children of God.

4. Be redeemed from the curse of the Law (Gal. 3:13): The Law of God exposes our sinfulness and condemns us, but Christ has redeemed us from the curse of the Law by becoming a curse for us on the cross.

5. Be resurrected and raptured to live together with him (I Th. 5:10): Those who belong to Christ will be raised to eternal life at the last day and will be with Him forever.

6. Be redeemed from iniquity, purified and zealous (Titus 2:14): Christ's sacrifice on the cross not only redeems us from the

penalty of sin, but also delivers us from its power. He purifies us and makes us zealous for good works.

7. Have an example to suffer patiently (I Pet. 2:21, 4:1; cp. I Jn. 3:16): Christ's suffering on the cross serves as an example for us to follow in our own sufferings. We are called to endure patiently and even to suffer for the sake of righteousness.

8. Be brought to God (I Pet. 3:18): Through Christ's sacrifice, we have been reconciled to God and brought into a right relationship with Him. He is the way, the truth, and the life, and no one comes to the Father except through Him.

What Do I Get When I am Saved?

1. Propitiation (Rom. 3:25): This refers to the satisfaction of God's righteous wrath against sin through the sacrifice of Jesus Christ on the cross. As a result, those who believe in Jesus are no longer under God's wrath and are instead reconciled to Him.

2. Justification (Rom. 5:9): This refers to the legal declaration that believers in Jesus are declared righteous before God because of their faith in Christ. This righteousness is not earned through good works but is a gift of God's grace.

3. Redemption (Eph. 1:7; cp. Acts 20:28; Col. 1:14; Heb. 9:12; I Pet. 1:19; Rev. 5:9): This refers to the payment of a price to purchase someone's freedom. Believers in Jesus have been redeemed from the penalty and power of sin through the sacrifice of Jesus Christ on the cross.

4. Intimacy with God (Eph. 2:13): This refers to the close relationship that believers in Jesus have with God. They are no longer separated from God because of their sin, but are now able to approach Him with confidence and enjoy fellowship with Him.

5. Forgiveness (Col. 1:14; Rev. 1:5): This refers to the cancellation of the debt of sin that believers in Jesus owe to God. Because of Jesus' sacrifice on the cross, believers are forgiven of their sins and are no longer under condemnation.

6. Reconciliation (peace)(Col. 1:20): This refers to the restoration of the broken relationship between God and humanity. Because of Jesus' sacrifice on the cross, believers in Jesus are now reconciled to God and can experience His peace.

7. Boldness in prayer (Heb. 10:19): This refers to the confidence that believers in Jesus can have when approaching God in prayer. Because of Jesus' sacrifice, they have access to God and can boldly bring their requests to Him.

8. Sanctification (Heb. 13:12; cp. Rev. 7:14): This refers to the process of becoming more like Christ. Believers in Jesus are set apart for God's purposes and are empowered by the Holy Spirit to live a holy life.

9. Power to overcome (Rev. 12:11): This refers to the strength and ability that believers in Jesus have to resist temptation and overcome sin. They are empowered by the Holy Spirit to live a victorious life and to stand against the attacks of the enemy.

Good work doesn't result in salvation, good work are the result of salvation.

- Good works do not earn salvation, but they are a result of salvation. We are saved by faith in Jesus Christ, not by our own good works (Ephesians 2:8-9).

- As believers, we are called to a new way of life. We are saved to live for God and to do good works that honor Him (Ephesians 2:10).

- Good works should flow out of our love for God and for others. We should seek to meet the urgent needs of others and to be productive in doing good (Titus 3:14).

- Through good works, we contribute to God's restoration of the world. We are called to build up, rather than tear down, and to make a positive impact on the lives of those around us.

- Good works are not a burden, but a privilege. They give us a sense of purpose and meaning, and they bring glory to God.

SALVATION AND BAPTISM

In the journey of faith, one of the most profound and transformative moments is the act of baptism. Baptism is a sacred and symbolic ritual that holds a special place in the hearts of Christians worldwide. It is not merely an external rite but a powerful expression of one's commitment to Christ, signifying the forgiveness of sins and the beginning of a new life in Him.

Baptism, often referred to as a "bath of regeneration," has been a subject of theological contemplation and a source of spiritual nourishment for believers throughout the ages. In this chapter, we delve into the depths of this sacred practice, exploring its significance in the context of salvation, the forgiveness of sins, and the restoration of our relationship with God through faith in Jesus Christ.

The Essence of Baptism

Before we can comprehend the importance of baptism in the context of salvation, we must first understand the essence of this sacred act. Baptism symbolizes a profound spiritual truth – the washing away of sin and the emergence of a new life in Christ. It is a tangible representation of the inner transformation that occurs when a person places their faith in Jesus.

Baptism in Christian tradition involves the submersion, sprinkling, or pouring of water, signifying purification and renewal. This practice has its roots in both the teachings of Jesus and the early Christian Church. For many Christians, baptism is a fundamental act of obedience, following the command of Christ in the Great Commission: "Go therefore and make disciples of all nations, baptizing them in the name of the Father and of the Son and of the Holy Spirit" (Matthew 28:19, ESV).

Salvation and Baptism

At the heart of the Christian faith lies the concept of salvation. It is the central message of the Gospel, a message of hope and redemption. Through faith in Jesus Christ, believers experience the forgiveness of their sins and are reconciled to God. Baptism plays an integral role in this process by publicly symbolizing the inner transformation that salvation brings.

Justification: In Christian theology, justification is a pivotal aspect of salvation. It refers to the act of God declaring a sinner as righteous through faith in Christ. Baptism is seen as the moment when this declaration is visibly enacted. As the believer is immersed in the water, it is as if their old, sin-stained self is buried, and they rise from the water as a new creation, justified before God. The act of baptism symbolizes the washing away of guilt and shame, as the believer's sins are forgiven.

Sanctification: Baptism is not only a declaration of justification but also marks the beginning of the sanctification process. Sanctification is the ongoing transformation and growth in holiness that occurs in the life of a believer. It is a lifelong journey of conforming to the image of Christ. Baptism serves as the starting point, symbolizing the believer's commitment to follow Jesus and allowing the Holy Spirit to work within them, molding them into His likeness.

Glorification: The ultimate goal of salvation is glorification – the state of being in the presence of God for all eternity. Baptism, while an earthly act, is a profound step towards that eternal destiny. It represents the believer's hope of resurrection and the promise of eternal life in Christ. In this sense, baptism is not an end but a glorious beginning of an everlasting journey with the Lord.

Baptism as a Profound Act of Faith

Baptism is a visible, outward expression of an inward faith in Christ. It is an act of obedience, symbolizing the believer's repentance from sin and the turning to Christ for salvation. The act of baptism is accompanied by a confession of faith, acknowledging Jesus as Lord and Savior.

Moreover, baptism is an act of humility. By entering the waters of baptism, the believer acknowledges their need for cleansing and forgiveness. It is a recognition that we cannot save ourselves, but through faith in Christ, we are made clean. Baptism is a powerful reminder of our dependence on God's grace and the transformative work of the Holy Spirit.

Baptism: A Community Affair

Baptism is not merely a personal experience; it is a communal one. It is an event celebrated within the church community and witnessed by fellow believers. In this sense, baptism is an act of unity within the body of Christ. It signifies the believer's identification with the larger family of faith, joining a community of fellow pilgrims on the journey of salvation.

The Mode of Baptism

Immersion baptism, conducted in the name of the Father, Son, and the Holy Spirit, holds profound significance for many Christian denominations. This mode of baptism, exemplified in the Bible with references like Matthew 28:19, involves fully immersing the believer in water, symbolizing spiritual truths of death to sin and resurrection to a new life in Christ.

In Matthew 28:19 (NIV), Jesus instructs his disciples, saying, "Therefore go and make disciples of all nations, baptizing them in the name of the Father and of the Son and of the Holy Spirit." This verse underscores the divine command to baptize in the triune name of God, highlighting the importance of immersion in the context of Christian baptism.

Immersing in water corresponds with the Apostle Paul's teachings in Romans 6:4, which state, "We were therefore buried with him through baptism into death in order that, just as Christ was raised from the dead through the glory of the Father, we too may live a new life." The act of immersion vividly illustrates the burial of the old self, steeped in sin, and the subsequent resurrection into a transformed existence, now united with Christ.

The emphasis on immersion baptism underscores the depth of the believer's commitment and the cleansing power of God's grace. Going beneath the water symbolizes the burial of one's sinful past and the emergence into a life renewed by faith in Christ. It aligns with the Christian understanding that through faith in Jesus, sins are washed away, and the believer is spiritually reborn.

Immersion baptism signifies a personal and public declaration of faith, akin to the symbolic act of dying and rising with Christ. This powerful and meaningful practice resonates with those seeking a profound connection with God and a visible representation of their Christian journey. In sum, immersion baptism in the name of the Father, Son, and Holy Spirit stands as a vivid expression of spiritual rebirth, cleansing, and a renewed life in Christ, deeply rooted in biblical and theological foundations.

Challenges to Baptism

In the rich tapestry of Christian tradition, there have been debates and differences of opinion regarding baptism. Some Christians place great importance on infant baptism, while others emphasize believer's baptism, where one must make a conscious decision to follow Christ before being baptized. These differing perspectives reflect the complexity and diversity of Christian theology. However, despite these differences, all Christians can unite in affirming the central importance of baptism in the context of salvation.

In the journey from sin to salvation, baptism stands as a pivotal milestone. It is a sacred act that signifies justification, sanctification, and the hope of glorification. Baptism is an expression of faith, a humbling acknowledgment of one's need for redemption, and a communal celebration of new life in Christ.

Baptism is more than a ritual; it is a profound act of obedience and devotion, symbolizing the inner transformation that takes place when one encounters the saving grace of Jesus. As believers step into the waters of baptism, they declare their allegiance to Christ and their trust in His redemptive work. Baptism is a powerful testimony of God's mercy and a testimony to the world that they have embraced the path to salvation.

Recently on the 25 November 2023 I baptised 18 people who decided to follow the Lord and serve Him through their life, after giving them the baptism I was sitting and I was suddenly reminded by myself that on this very day 18 years ago on 25 November 2005 I was baptised by my father in Sundargarh and 18 years later I am baptising 18 people in a different part of Odisha and I think that is the journey of salvation, salvation is personal but salvation is never selfish if you are saved you will never want somebody to die without getting saved.

"Saving Souls For Eternity"

While salvation is inherently a deeply personal encounter, its transformative power is never meant to be selfish. At the core of the Christian faith is an irrepressible desire to share the life-transforming message of Christ. It is a conviction that if you have discovered the path to salvation, you would earnestly desire that others do not perish without encountering this redeeming grace. The act of baptizing 18 individuals precisely 18 years after my own baptism stands as a testament to the perpetuating ripple effect of salvation—a journey initiated by a personal encounter with God's grace and perpetuated by a passionate commitment to share that grace with others.

Discipleship: Fulfilling the Great Commission (Matthew 28:19-20):

The Great Commission, by Jesus Himself in Matthew 28:19-20, is a divine mandate for every believer. It is a call to make disciples, baptize them, and teach them to observe all that Jesus commanded. Discipleship is the heartbeat of Christianity, the active pursuit of

Christlikeness, and the intentional investment in the spiritual growth of others.

Understanding the Need for Discipleship:

The need for discipleship is underscored by the understanding that conversion is just the beginning of the journey. Baptism marks the initiation, but true discipleship is a lifelong commitment to walk alongside fellow believers, guiding them in the transformative journey of becoming more like Christ. The Great Commission emphasizes not just making believers but nurturing mature followers of Christ.

The Threefold Mandate:

1. **Make Disciples:** Discipleship begins with the intentional act of making disciples. It involves sharing the message of salvation, leading people to encounter Christ, and helping them understand the transformative power of His grace.

2. **Baptize Them:** Baptism is the public declaration of one's faith, a symbol of identification with Christ's death, burial, and resurrection. Through baptism, disciples publicly announce their commitment to Christ, signifying a radical transformation within.

3. **Teach Them:** The journey doesn't end with baptism; it extends to the ongoing process of teaching and learning. Discipleship involves instructing believers in the ways of Christ, imparting spiritual wisdom, and nurturing a deep understanding of God's Word.

The Ongoing Commitment:

Discipleship is not a one-time event but an ongoing commitment. It's about walking together through the highs and lows of the Christian journey, providing support, encouragement, and accountability. It's a relational investment that mirrors the way Jesus discipled His followers during His earthly ministry.

The Joy of Multiplication:

The beauty of discipleship is its inherent multiplication factor. A disciple, having been nurtured and equipped, becomes a disciple-maker. This multiplication effect is at the heart of the Great Commission's transformative power. As disciples make disciples, the impact spreads exponentially, creating a vibrant community of believers who are deeply rooted in Christ and passionately committed to His mission.

In essence, the journey from sin to salvation finds a pivotal marker in baptism, and discipleship becomes the guiding principle for those who have embraced the transformative power of Christ. As we fulfill the Great Commission, making disciples, baptizing them, and teaching them, we participate in a divine legacy of spiritual multiplication—a legacy that perpetuates the profound joy of salvation from one generation to the next.

Chapter 6
The Guiding Spirit: Understanding the Role of the Holy Spirit

The Holy Spirit, an indispensable component of the Christian faith, beckons us to embark on a profound exploration of His identity and the pivotal role He assumes in our lives. This quest extends beyond a mere intellectual pursuit, as it stands as a cornerstone for our spiritual maturation and advancement.

Billy Graham, a venerable figure in Christian ministry, encapsulates the essence of the Holy Spirit's influence by asserting, "The Holy Spirit illuminates the minds of people, makes us yearn for God, and takes spiritual truth and makes it understandable to us." Such wisdom reinforces that our comprehension of the Holy Spirit is not confined to doctrinal study but is a transformative force that aligns our hearts with the divine.

Within the intricate tapestry of God's being, the Holy Spirit emerges as a magnificent and indispensable facet. His presence empowers us to fathom our true potential and navigate the complexities of life. Stripped of the Spirit's guidance, we find ourselves bereft of strength and direction. Yet, through His indwelling strength, we are bestowed with the capacity to overcome any obstacle.

In contemporary times, amidst the proliferation of false prophets and misleading teachings, a lamentable trend has emerged. The

Holy Spirit, rather than being revered with reverence, is often trivialized. In regions like India, a surge in so-called deliverance and healing ministries has given rise to practices that reduce the sacred presence of the Holy Spirit to commercial transactions. Individuals peddle water, oil, or even soap, claiming that these commodities induce manifestations of the Holy Spirit. Such endeavors not only misconstrue the biblical teachings but also turn the sacred into a commodity for personal gain.

In the face of these distortions, it becomes imperative for believers to discern the true nature of the Holy Spirit. This chapter will unravel the authentic biblical understanding of the Holy Spirit, steering us away from the mockery of His sacred presence and guiding us toward a genuine, transformative relationship with the third person of the Trinity.

The Holy Spirit is a divine and essential member of the triune Godhead. Here are some key points to understand about the Holy Spirit:

- The Holy Spirit convicts us of our sin and shows us our need for a Savior. He makes us aware of the judgment that is coming to those who reject Jesus Christ (John 16:8-11).

- When we repent of our sin and receive Jesus Christ as our Savior, the Holy Spirit regenerates our dead spirit, making it alive to the things of God (John 3:1-16; Acts 2:38).

- There is a second work of the Holy Spirit called the baptism of the Holy Spirit, which is available to all believers (Acts 2:1-4). This is a gift of empowerment that enables us to live a holy life and fulfill the will of God.

- The primary purpose of the baptism of the Holy Spirit is to empower us to witness to others (Acts 1:8). Through the Holy

Spirit's help, we become more like Jesus and are directed to do the Father's will.

- The Holy Spirit is our Helper and Guide, who comforts us, teaches us, and leads us into all truth (John 14:16-17, 26; 16:13).

- The Holy Spirit gives us spiritual gifts for the building up of the church and the advancement of God's kingdom (1 Corinthians 12:4-11).

- The Holy Spirit produces fruit in our lives, such as love, joy, peace, patience, kindness, goodness, faithfulness, gentleness, and self-control (Galatians 5:22-23).

- We are called to be filled with the Holy Spirit, which means being continually empowered and directed by Him (Ephesians 5:18). This requires surrendering to God's will, being obedient to His Word, and walking in fellowship with Him.

HOLY SPIRIT CAN START WITH AN ENCOUNTER AND TURN YOUR LIFE INTO A LIVING EXPERIENCE.

The Holy Spirit is an essential part of the Christian faith, and as believers, we should seek to have a close relationship with Him. There are several ways in which the Holy Spirit can impact our lives and make us more like Christ.

Firstly, we are encouraged to ask the Holy Spirit to fill us up regularly. This means asking Him to come and dwell within us, to empower us and guide us in all situations. As believers, we can easily become depleted and feel weak, but when we ask the Holy Spirit to replenish us, we can experience His strength and power in our lives.

Secondly, the Holy Spirit is our Helper. He is always with us, guiding us and directing us in the way we should go. In John 16:7, Jesus tells His disciples that it is better for Him to go away so that the Helper (the Holy Spirit) can come and be with them. The Holy Spirit is there to comfort us, to teach us, and to lead us into all truth.

Thirdly, the Holy Spirit sanctifies us. This means that He sets us apart for God's purposes and helps us to become more like Christ. In 1 Corinthians 6:11, Paul reminds us that we were washed, sanctified, and justified in the name of the Lord Jesus Christ and by the Spirit of our God. The Holy Spirit works in us to produce the fruit of the Spirit (Galatians 5:22-23) and to transform us into the image of Christ (2 Corinthians 3:18).

THE EXPERIENCE AND THE EMPOWERMENT OF THE HOLY SPIRIT IN OUR LIVES

1. The Holy Spirit helps you to do the Father's will - As believers, we are called to live according to God's will. However, it can be challenging to discern what that means in our daily lives. The Holy Spirit serves as our guide, helping us to know and understand what God wants us to do. In Acts 8:29, the Holy Spirit directed Philip to approach the Ethiopian eunuch and share the gospel with him.

2. The Holy Spirit gifts you for ministry - The Holy Spirit imparts spiritual gifts to believers to empower them for ministry. These gifts can be used to build up the body of Christ and advance His Kingdom. In 1 Corinthians 12:4-11, we see examples of spiritual gifts such as prophecy, healing, and speaking in tongues.

3. The Holy Spirit imparts love - The Holy Spirit fills us with God's love, allowing us to love others selflessly. Romans 5:3-5 tells

us that the Holy Spirit pours God's love into our hearts, giving us the ability to love even our enemies.

4. The Holy Spirit gives hope - The Holy Spirit provides us with hope, even in the midst of difficult circumstances. Romans 15:13 says that the Holy Spirit fills us with joy and peace as we trust in God, giving us hope for the future.

5. The Holy Spirit teaches and gives insight - The Holy Spirit serves as our teacher and guide, illuminating God's Word and helping us to understand it. John 14:26 tells us that the Holy Spirit will teach us all things and bring to our remembrance everything that Jesus taught.

6. The Holy Spirit guides your prayers - Sometimes we may not know what to pray or how to pray for a specific situation. The Holy Spirit intercedes for us and guides our prayers according to God's will. Romans 8:26 says that the Holy Spirit helps us in our weakness and intercedes for us with groanings that cannot be expressed in words.

7. The Holy Spirit uses you for evangelism - The Holy Spirit empowers us to be witnesses for Christ and share the gospel with others. In Acts 1:8, Jesus promised that the Holy Spirit would come upon His disciples and they would be His witnesses, both in Jerusalem and in all Judea and Samaria, and to the ends of the earth.

The proof of the Baptism of the Holy Spirit:

1. The gift of the Holy Spirit - 1 Corinthians 12:7-11: One of the clear signs of the Baptism of the Holy Spirit is the manifestation of spiritual gifts that are given to believers for the common good. These gifts include but are not limited to speaking in tongues, prophecy, healing, miracles, and discernment of spirits.

The Holy Spirit distributes these gifts as He wills, and they are given to help build up the body of Christ and advance God's kingdom.

2. The Fruit of the Holy Spirit - Galatians 5:22-23: The Baptism of the Holy Spirit also bears fruit in the life of the believer. The fruit of the Holy Spirit is evidence of the inward work that the Spirit is doing in our hearts, and it includes love, joy, peace, patience, kindness, goodness, faithfulness, gentleness, and self-control. These are qualities that are produced in us as we yield to the Holy Spirit's guidance and allow Him to work in and through us.

3. Changed lives and transformed behavior: Another proof of the Baptism of the Holy Spirit is a transformed life and behavior. The Holy Spirit empowers us to live a life that is pleasing to God, and He helps us to overcome sin and temptation. As we yield to the Holy Spirit, we become more like Christ, and our lives become a testimony of His grace and power at work in us.

4. Increased hunger for God's Word and prayer: Another sign of the Baptism of the Holy Spirit is an increased hunger for God's Word and prayer. The Holy Spirit illuminates the Scriptures, helping us to understand and apply them to our lives. He also gives us a deep desire to spend time in prayer and fellowship with God, and to seek His will in all things.

5. Boldness to share the gospel: The Baptism of the Holy Spirit also gives us boldness to share the gospel with others. The Holy Spirit empowers us to be witnesses for Christ, to boldly proclaim His truth, and to share His love with those around us. He also gives us the words to say and the courage to speak up when the opportunity arises.

Living in the Spirit means allowing the Holy Spirit to guide and direct our lives, rather than relying on our own strength and understanding. Here are some key points to expand on this idea:

1. Romans 8:1-17: This passage explains that those who live according to the flesh will experience death, but those who live according to the Spirit will have life and peace. Living in the Spirit means setting our minds on the things of the Spirit and submitting to the Spirit's leading. This results in transformation, as we become more like Christ and experience the fullness of our adoption as children of God.

2. Galatians 5:16: This verse tells us to walk in the Spirit so that we will not gratify the desires of the flesh. When we live in the Spirit, we are able to resist temptation and overcome sin. We are empowered to love and serve others selflessly, rather than being consumed by selfish desires.

3. 2 Corinthians 3:17: This verse tells us that where the Spirit of the Lord is, there is freedom. Living in the Spirit means experiencing freedom from the power of sin and death, and being able to live in the fullness of the abundant life that Jesus offers.

4. 2 Corinthians 12:9: This verse reminds us that the power of the Holy Spirit is made perfect in our weakness. Living in the Spirit means acknowledging our own weakness and relying on the strength of the Spirit to sustain us and guide us through all circumstances.

Overall, living in the Spirit means surrendering our own will and desires to the will of God and allowing the Holy Spirit to lead us into a life of obedience and fruitfulness. It means experiencing the transformative power of God's love and grace, and being empowered to fulfil our calling to love and serve others in the name of Jesus.

THE HOLY SPIRIT STARTS IN US WITH AN ENCOUNTER AND STAYS IN US TO EMPOWER

Chapter 7

Conversing with the Divine: The Power and Importance of Prayer

PRAYER HAS NO POWER, THERE IS POWER IN THE NAME OF JESUS ! – BENNY HINN ,

This statement is as powerful as it sounds, I was watching Benny Hinn recently in a YouTube video and ears got opened really wide when I heard him say there's no power in prayer, I replayed it again to hear him loud and clear and he said there's no power in prayer because Hindus pray, Muslims pray, and all the other religions pray but many a times it also goes unanswered because the power is in the name of Jesus alone.

Prayer is a vital aspect of the Christian life and has immense importance for a believer. Prayer is essential for the Christian life as it helps us to connect with God, deepen our faith, seek guidance, find peace, gain spiritual strength, intercede for others, foster humility and align us with God's will.

The beauty of a Christocentric prayer lies in its accessibility. Unlike many human interactions that may be confined by physical locations, prayer transcends such limitations. It's a divine conversation that doesn't necessitate a particular setting for God to hear our hearts. "In the profound depths of life's darkest corners, there is no shadow so dense that God cannot hear your prayers when uttered with a sincere heart."

In essence, prayer is a direct line of communication with the Almighty, and this connection is not bound by the constraints of geography or specific spaces. Whether you're in the solitude of your room, amidst the beauty of nature, or even in the midst of life's chaotic moments, prayer remains a constant. It's an intimate dialogue that can unfold anywhere, at any time.

In 2012, I embarked on a journey to establish a prayer group named "Prayer Ryderz", driven by a vision to intercede for our cities while riding motorcycles because one of my hobby back then was doing long motorbike rides and praying for each city that I pass through. Our mission was simple yet profound: to pray for the welfare and spiritual upliftment of our communities. We would set out on our bikes, traversing the bustling streets, and amidst the roar of engines, we lifted our voices in prayer.

Stopping at roadside tea stalls, we would gather for impromptu Bible talks, sharing God's word and encouraging one another in faith. These moments were sacred, amidst the hustle and bustle of city life, as we found solace and strength in the presence of God.

Through Prayer Ryderz, we witnessed the transformative power of prayer unleashed in unexpected places. It taught us that prayer knows no boundaries, transcending the limitations of physical space. Whether on the open road or gathered around a humble tea stall, our prayers reverberated with divine resonance, touching hearts and transforming lives.

This experience affirmed the truth that prayer is not confined to sacred spaces or quiet corners but can permeate every aspect of our lives, infusing even the most ordinary moments with divine significance. It's a testament to the unyielding power of prayer to shape our destinies and bring about God's kingdom on earth.

This universality of prayer reflects the omnipresence of God—His ability to be present everywhere simultaneously. It's a reassuring truth that allows believers to commune with their Creator in moments of joy, sorrow, solitude, or community. So, whether you find yourself in a grand cathedral, a humble home, or beneath the open sky, the invitation to prayer remains ever open.

In the simplicity of a whispered prayer or the solemnity of a heartfelt cry, God listens. The sincerity of our hearts matters more than the grandeur of our surroundings. Thus, the sacredness of prayer lies not in a specific location but in the genuine connection between the Creator and the created.

In the tapestry of Christian life, prayer emerges as a vital thread, intricately woven to connect us with the divine. It serves as a sacred avenue for deepening our faith, seeking divine guidance, finding profound peace, gaining spiritual fortitude, interceding fervently for others, fostering humility, and aligning our desires with the sovereign will of God.

The recognition that the real power lies not in the mere act of praying but in the specific invocation of the name of Jesus becomes a guiding principle in my prayer life. Each sacred conversation becomes an acknowledgment of the transformative power resident in the name that is above all names — the name of Jesus Christ. This revelation elevates prayer from a routine to a revelation, emphasizing the unique authority inherent in the name of Jesus.

So, as we journey through the exploration of prayer in this chapter, let us unveil the profound reality that our prayers derive their efficacy, not from a generic act, but from the invocation of the name that carries unparalleled power — the name of Jesus.

What is Prayer for us ?

1. Communication with God: Prayer is a way to talk to God, to communicate with Him, to share our thoughts and emotions, and to express our desires to Him.

2. Two-way communication: Prayer is not just a monologue where we speak to God and He listens. It is a two-way communication where we speak to God, and He speaks to us. We can hear His voice through His Word, His Spirit, and the circumstances of our lives.

3. Relationship with God: Prayer is essential for building and maintaining a healthy relationship with God. Just as communication is crucial for any relationship, so it is for our relationship with God.

4. Spiritual growth: Prayer is a means of spiritual growth. Through prayer, we can grow in our faith, our knowledge of God, and our love for Him.

5. Fellowship with God: Prayer is a way of fellowshipping with God. Through prayer, we can experience His presence, His love, His grace, and His power.

6. Submission to God: Prayer is a way of submitting to God's will. As we pray, we can surrender our desires to His will and seek His guidance and direction for our lives.

7. Intercession: Prayer is a way of interceding for others. Through prayer, we can lift up the needs and concerns of others before God and ask for His intervention in their lives.

8. Spiritual warfare: Prayer is a powerful weapon in spiritual warfare. Through prayer, we can resist the enemy's attacks, overcome temptations, and claim victory in Christ.

9. Thanksgiving: Prayer is a way of expressing our gratitude to God for all His blessings and provision in our lives. We can thank Him for His faithfulness, His goodness, His mercy, and His grace.

10. Obedience: Prayer is a way of seeking God's will and obeying His commands. As we pray, we can ask for the strength and guidance to follow Him faithfully and fulfill His purposes for our lives.

Prayer is Telling	**Prayer is Listening**
Psalm 145:18-19 - The Lord hears our cries	1 Samuel 3:1-14 - Samuel listens to God's voice
Jeremiah 33:3 - God promises to answer our call	1 Samuel 3:10 - Samuel responds to God's call
Proverbs 15:29 - God hears the prayers of righteous	Hebrew word "shâmaʻ" means to hear intelligently

Prayer is a two-way communication, both talking and listening. When we pray, we can tell God our emotions and desires, knowing that He hears our cries and promises to answer our call. At the same time, we can listen to God's voice and respond to His call, just as Samuel did in the Old Testament. The Hebrew word "shâmaʻ" emphasizes the importance of listening intelligently, with attention and obedience. Many a times what happens we have a list of our wishes for God to be fulfilled, as if He is a Gini who is here with some magical power who will fulfil the desire of our matter if that is good or bad for us. Its not like that God is a sensible Father and He knows what is the best for us and when it's the right time anything in our lives, He is also a Friends who likes to speak to us without being judgemental of your situation but sadly we don't have any time left in our prayers to listen from Him because we busy only in speaking. We say Thy will be done in our prayers but never have the time listen to His will for our lives. Since 2017 I changed the way for prayers and it has effectively changed by life style because since I have the style where I speak less and listen more in prayer because the One who is speaking to knows more about me and situation better than me. Sometime all you need is the words spoken by Samuel that night "Speak Lord, your servant is listen" this is the most powerful you can do sometime in your circumstances and it will be enough because you will understand more about God's presences and sovereignty in your circumstances . As we practice both telling and listening in prayer, we can deepen our fellowship with God and grow in our faith.

"MORE LISTENING, LESS SPEAKING"

When we pray, it is essential to approach God with a sincere and genuine heart. Jesus warns us against hypocrisy in prayer, as He did to the religious leaders who used public prayers for personal gain and praise. Therefore, our prayers must be real, honest, and heartfelt.

Jesus taught us to pray in Matthew 6:5-14, commonly known as the Lord's Prayer. He provided a model for how we should pray, beginning with acknowledging God's holiness and authority and seeking His will. Jesus also emphasized the importance of forgiveness, both seeking and offering it.

In addition to following Jesus' model prayer, we must also pray in faith, believing that God hears us and answers our prayers according to His will. James 1:6-7 instructs us to ask in faith, without doubting, for the one who doubts is like a wave of the sea, driven and tossed by the wind.

Prayer must also be persistent, as Jesus encourages us to ask, seek, and knock, and we will receive, find, and have doors opened to us (Matthew 7:7-8). We should pray continually and not give up, trusting that God hears and answers our prayers in His perfect timing.

Prayer must be accompanied by a life of obedience and surrender to God. We cannot live in disobedience and expect our prayers to be answered. As we seek God's will and surrender our lives to Him, we can have confidence that He hears and answers our prayers.

ACTS and I can be used to remember five key themes in Christian prayer:

1. Adoration - Praising God for who He is and what He has done. This can involve acknowledging His character traits, such as love, mercy, and grace, and expressing gratitude for His blessings. Using the acronym, you can start your prayer with words of adoration like "Dear God, I know that you are all-loving and merciful."

2. Confession - Admitting your sins and asking for forgiveness. Confession is an important aspect of prayer as it helps to keep you accountable and honest with God. To incorporate confession in your prayers, you can say something like, "Please forgive me for the horrible things I have said about...".

3. Thanksgiving - Expressing gratitude for the blessings and good things in your life. This can include thanking God for His provision, protection, and guidance. You can thank God for anything from small things like good weather to big things like family and friends. Using the acronym, you can start your prayer with words of thanksgiving like "Thank you for the amazing weather this week."

4. Supplication - Asking God for help, strength, or guidance. Supplication is an important part of prayer as it allows you to bring your needs and requests before God. This can include asking for God's grace to help with something, such as "Give me strength to overcome this challenge."

5. Intercession - Praying for others who are in need. Intercession involves asking God to help and bless others, such as praying for a sick friend or a struggling family member. You can intercede for anyone, even people you don't know personally. To incorporate intercession in your prayers, you can say something like, "Please remember my cousin, who is ill, and help them to heal after their operation."

By using the ACTS acronym, you can structure your prayers and remember to include all five key themes. This can help to ensure that your prayers are well-rounded, and that you're not just asking for things, but also praising God and expressing gratitude.

Speaking in tongues, also known as praying in the Spirit, is a spiritual gift that is given to some believers according to 1 Corinthians 12:10. There are four primary Scripture passages that are cited as evidence for this gift: Romans 8:26; 1 Corinthians 14:4-17; Ephesians 6:18; and Jude verse 20.

Romans 8:26 teaches us that when we are weak and do not know what to pray for, the Holy Spirit helps us by interceding for us with groans that words cannot express. This is evidence that the Spirit can pray through us in a language that we may not understand, which is often referred to as speaking in tongues.

In 1 Corinthians 14:4-17, Paul instructs the church in Corinth to pursue the gift of speaking in tongues, and explains that when we pray in tongues, our spirit is praying to God, even though our mind may not understand what is being said. This suggests that speaking in tongues is a legitimate form of prayer that can be beneficial to believers.

Ephesians 6:18 and Jude 20 mention "praying in the Spirit," which is often understood to refer to speaking in tongues. The phrase "praying in the Spirit" implies that we are praying in a way that is guided by the Holy Spirit, and speaking in tongues is one way that the Spirit can lead us in prayer.

While it is true that Romans 8:26 states that it is the Spirit who "groans," not believers, and that the "groans" of the Spirit "cannot be expressed," this does not necessarily negate the idea of speaking in tongues as a form of prayer. Rather, it suggests that the Spirit can pray through us in a way that transcends our understanding and our ability to articulate with words.

while there are varying interpretations of the passages related to speaking in tongues, it is clear that the Bible acknowledges this as a legitimate form of prayer and a gift of the Holy Spirit. When we pray in the Spirit, we are allowing the Holy Spirit to guide our prayers and to intercede for us in a way that goes beyond our human understanding. This can be a powerful and transformative experience, as we surrender ourselves to the leading of the Spirit and allow God to work in us in a deeper way.

While the practice of speaking in tongues is sometimes controversial and misunderstood, it is a legitimate spiritual gift that is given to some believers. Those who practice speaking in tongues believe that it is a way to connect with God on a deeper level and to allow the Holy Spirit to work through them in a powerful way.

It is important to note that speaking in tongues is not the only way to pray in the Spirit, and it is not necessary for every believer to practice this form of prayer. However, for those who feel called to this practice, it can be a deeply meaningful and transformative way to connect with God and to allow the Holy Spirit to work in their lives.

The Bible teaches that prayer must be done in accordance with God's will and in alignment with His Word.

In 1 John 5:14-15, we read, "And this is the confidence that we have toward him, that if we ask anything according to his will he hears us. And if we know that he hears us in whatever we ask, we know that we have the requests that we have asked of him." This passage emphasizes the importance of praying according to God's will, rather than our own desires. When we pray in alignment with God's will, we can have confidence that our prayers will be heard and answered.

James 4:3 also warns against praying with selfish motives. It says, "You ask and do not receive, because you ask wrongly, to spend it on your passions." This verse reminds us that prayer is not about seeking our own will, but about seeking to align ourselves with the will of God more fully.

Praying in accordance with God's Word is also important. The Bible is the source of God's wisdom and guidance, and when we pray in line with its teachings, we are more likely to be praying in accordance with God's will. This means that we should take the time to study and understand the Bible, so that we can pray in accordance with its teachings.

In conclusion, the key to answered prayer is praying in accordance with the will of God and in alignment with His Word. This means seeking to understand and align ourselves with God's will, rather than seeking our own desires. When we pray in this way, we can have confidence that our prayers will be heard and answered by a loving and faithful God.

The key to answered prayer is praying according to

the will of God and in accordance with His Word.

Chapter 8
Fasting for Spiritual Growth: Harnessing the Power of Abstinence

Fasting is a powerful and important spiritual discipline that has been practiced by believers for thousands of years. It involves abstaining from food, drink, or other activities for a specific period of time, in order to seek God's will, deepen one's relationship with Him, and gain spiritual insights and breakthroughs. In today's fast-paced and often spiritually-distracted world, the practice of fasting is more important than ever before because *fasting isn't the absence of anything it's the fullness in the closeness of God.*

Contrary to the prevalent misconception that fasting is synonymous with mere physical hunger or deprivation, it is imperative to recognize that its true essence lies in the richness of spiritual closeness with the divine. Fasting isn't a mere absence; it is a deliberate presence, a purposeful drawing near to the sacred source of life.

The contemporary narrative often reduces fasting to a mere act of staying hungry, overlooking the deeper, transformative dimensions it holds. True fasting, however, is a holistic experience that engages not only the physical but also the spiritual and emotional facets of our being. It transcends the mere denial of food or indulgence; it is an intentional pilgrimage into the realms of spiritual fullness.

In a world where the clamor for instant gratification and quick fixes prevails, fasting emerges as a counter-cultural practice that challenges the prevailing narrative. It invites us to pause amidst the relentless rush, to delve into the profound fullness found in the closeness of God. The modern mindset, often fixated on the physical aspects, misses the invitation to a deeper, more profound feast — a feast of spiritual abundance, communion, and transformative encounters.

The discipline of fasting, in its authentic form, is a symphony of the physical, spiritual, and emotional dimensions of our existence. It is a deliberate engagement with the divine, a conscious choice to abstain not only from physical indulgences but also from the noise that clutters our spiritual perception.

In Christianity, fasting is often viewed as a form of spiritual discipline and an act of devotion to God. It is seen as a way to deepen one's relationship with God and align one's will with His.

In the Bible, fasting is mentioned numerous times, with many stories of individuals and communities who fasted for spiritual reasons. Jesus himself fasted for 40 days in the wilderness before beginning his public ministry, and he taught his followers about the importance of fasting as a way to draw closer to God.

In the New Testament, fasting is often linked with prayer, as a way to intensify one's focus and create space for deeper communion with God. Christians may fast as individuals or as a community, for a specific period of time or as a regular practice.

The purpose of fasting in Christianity is not to earn favor or blessings from God, but rather to humbly submit oneself to God's will and seek His guidance and direction. It is seen as a way to cultivate a spirit of repentance, gratitude, and dependence on God.

Overall, fasting is an important spiritual discipline in Christianity that can help believers deepen their relationship with God, align their hearts with His will, and cultivate a spirit of humility and surrender. The essence of Christian fasting is not rooted in a transactional pursuit of blessings but in the profound submission to God's will. It's a sacred journey that cultivates repentance, gratitude, and an unwavering dependence on the Divine. Through fasting, believers are invited to a spiritual feast — a banquet of humility, surrender, and a deepening connection with the Creator.

As I navigate the sacred discipline of fasting, I am reminded that it is not a mere ritual; it's a sacred dialogue, a dance of the soul with the divine. In each moment of restraint, in every deliberate act of drawing closer to God, I find a profound fullness — a richness discovered in the intimate closeness of the One who satisfies the deepest longings of the human heart.

Why We Fast ?

1. Fasting Makes You Humble

Yes, fasting can indeed be a humbling experience, as it requires one to set aside their own desires and needs in order to focus on their relationship with God. When one fasts, they are forced to confront their own limitations and vulnerabilities, and to rely on God for sustenance and strength.

As mentioned in Psalms 35:13, David is described as humbling himself with fasting. In the Bible, there are numerous examples of individuals who fasted as a way to humble themselves before God, including Esther, Ezra, and Daniel.

Moreover, the act of fasting itself can be seen as an expression of humility, as it involves acknowledging one's own limitations and weaknesses, and seeking God's strength and guidance in the face of them. By fasting, one is reminded of their own mortality and dependence on God, and is encouraged to seek Him with a spirit of humility and reverence.

In this way, fasting can be a powerful tool for cultivating a deeper sense of humility and surrender to God. By setting aside one's own desires and needs, and focusing solely on God, believers can gain a greater perspective on their place in the world and their relationship with the divine.

2. Fasting gives you the RIGHT DIRECTION in ministry.

Yes, fasting can be a powerful tool for gaining clarity and direction in ministry. As mentioned in Matthew 4:1-2, Jesus himself fasted for 40 days in the wilderness before beginning his public ministry. During this time of fasting and prayer, Jesus was able to gain clarity on God's plan for his life and ministry, and to overcome the temptations of the devil.

In fact, throughout the Bible, there are numerous examples of individuals who fasted as a way to seek guidance and direction from God. For example, the prophet Daniel fasted and prayed for 21 days in order to receive a vision from God (Daniel 10:2-3).

When we fast, we are able to quiet our minds and bodies and create space for God to speak to us. By setting aside our physical desires and focusing solely on God, we are better able to discern His will for our lives and ministry.

Moreover, the act of fasting can also help us to develop a greater sense of discipline and self-control, which can be useful in our ministries. By learning to resist the temptation to give in to our physical desires, we can develop a stronger sense of spiritual fortitude and resilience, which can help us to withstand the challenges and obstacles that we may face in our ministries.

Overall, fasting can be a powerful tool for gaining direction and clarity in ministry, and for developing the spiritual strength and resilience that we need to carry out God's will in our lives.

3. Fasting gives you the POWER TO EMPOWER OTHERS.

In Acts 13:3, we see an example of how fasting can give believers the power to empower others for ministry. In this passage, the church in Antioch is described as fasting and praying before commissioning Paul and Barnabas for their missionary journey. The believers recognized the importance of seeking God's guidance and empowerment before sending these young disciples out into the world for ministry.

Through their time of fasting and prayer, the believers in Antioch were able to deepen their relationship with God and gain a greater sense of spiritual strength and empowerment. This enabled them to not only carry out their own ministries effectively but also to empower and support others in their ministries.

Moreover, fasting can help us to develop a greater sensitivity to the Holy Spirit and to discern God's will for our lives and ministries. By setting aside our own desires and focusing solely on God, we can open ourselves up to His guidance and direction, and allow Him to lead us in empowering others for His kingdom.

Furthermore, the discipline of fasting can help us to cultivate a spirit of selflessness and sacrifice, which is essential for effective ministry. By learning to deny our own desires and needs, we can better serve and support others in their ministries, and work together more effectively as a community of believers. Fasting can be a powerful tool for empowering believers for ministry, enabling us to deepen our relationship with God, discern His will, and support and empower others for the great commission. By setting aside our own desires and focusing solely on God, we can gain the spiritual strength and empowerment that we need to carry out His work in the world.

Types of Fasting

1. Regular Fasting: This type of fasting is commonly practiced in many religious traditions, including Christianity. It involves abstaining from all food and drinks except for water for a specific period of time. This type of fast is often used for spiritual reasons, such as seeking guidance from God, repentance, or spiritual renewal.

2. Partial Fasting: This type of fasting involves abstaining from certain types of food or drink for a specific period of time. Examples of partial fasting include abstaining from meat, sweets, or alcohol. Daniel practiced a partial fast in the Bible, where he ate only vegetables and drank only water for a specific period of time.

3. Absolute Fasting: This type of fasting involves abstaining from all food and liquid, including water, for a specific period of time. This type of fast is not recommended for extended periods of time and should only be practiced under the supervision of a medical professional. In the Bible, Esther, Ezra, and Saul all practiced absolute fasting for short periods of time.

4. Supernatural Fasting: This type of fasting is enabled only by a miraculous intervention from God. Moses practiced this type of fast when he went without food or water for 40 days on Mount

Sinai while receiving the Ten Commandments from God. This type of fast is not commonly practiced today, as it requires a direct intervention from God.

The type of fast chosen will depend on individual beliefs, circumstances, and health considerations.

There are other types of fasting that a Christian can do besides fasting from food and drink. These can include:

1. Screen time fasting: Abstaining from the use of electronic devices such as smartphones, laptops, and televisions for a designated period of time to refocus on God.

2. Social media fasting: Abstaining from the use of social media platforms such as Facebook, Instagram, Twitter, etc. for a certain period of time to spend more time in prayer and reading the Bible.

3. Entertainment fasting: Abstaining from engaging in certain forms of entertainment, such as movies, music, and video games, to dedicate more time to spiritual activities.

4. Sexual fasting: Abstaining from sexual activities for a certain period of time, as a form of self-control and to focus on spiritual growth.

5. Solitude fasting: Setting aside a specific period of time to be alone with God, away from distractions and the busyness of life, to seek His guidance and presence.

These types of fasts can help Christians to grow closer to God, gain clarity and direction in their lives, and develop self-discipline and self-control. It's important to seek God's guidance before embarking on any type of fast and to make sure that the focus is on seeking God, rather than simply depriving oneself of something.

Length of Fasting

1. One Day or Part of the Day Fasting - The Bible provides examples of fasting for one day or part of the day, such as in Judges 20:26, 1 Samuel 7:6, 2 Samuel 1:12; 3:35, Nehemiah 9:1, and Jeremiah 36:6. This type of fasting can be a good starting point for beginners or those who have never fasted before.

2. One Night Fasting - Daniel 6:18-24 gives an example of fasting for one night. This could involve skipping dinner or fasting from sunset to sunrise.

3. Three Days Fasting - Esther 4:16 and Acts 9:9 give examples of fasting for three days. This type of fast can be challenging but also achievable for many people.

4. Seven Days Fasting - 1 Samuel 31:13 and 2 Samuel 12:16-23 provide examples of fasting for seven days. This type of fast is longer and may require more preparation and guidance from the Holy Spirit.

5. Fourteen Days Fasting - Acts 27:33-34 tells of a fast for fourteen days during a shipwreck. This type of fast can be very challenging, and it is essential to seek guidance from the Holy Spirit and medical advice if necessary.

6. Twenty-one Days of Fasting - Daniel 10:3-13 gives an example of fasting for twenty-one days. This type of fast requires discipline and guidance from the Holy Spirit, and it can be a time of intense spiritual growth.

7. Forty Days Fasting of Jesus - Finally, the Bible tells us of Jesus' forty-day fast in the wilderness (Matthew 4:2, Luke 4:2). This type of fast requires significant preparation, guidance, and medical advice.

Ultimately, the length of a fast should be determined by the individual's physical health and guidance from the Holy Spirit. Fasting is not a competition, but a personal discipline that should be approached with reverence and humility.

Fasting should be viewed as a means of drawing closer to God and seeking His guidance rather than as a tool for manipulating outcomes in our favor. It is important to remember that God already knows our wants and needs, and that He will never abandon us in our times of need. Therefore, we should not misuse the power of fasting for personal gain or selfish motives. Instead, we should approach it with reverence and use it wisely, as it has the potential to bring about significant transformations in our lives.

Chapter 9

The Freedom of Forgiveness: Unlocking Its Healing Power

Unforgiveness has become a lethal tool in today's world, causing division and discord within the Christian community. However, the Agape Love of God is the most powerful weapon against unforgiveness, capable of forgiving everything. As Mahatma Gandhi once said, "Forgiveness is the attribute of the strong, and the weak can never forgive." Forgiveness should begin with a change of heart and culminate in actions that have the power to transform the hearts of those we are forgiving or seeking forgiveness from.

Growing up in India we used to watch movie sometime on the TVs most of the movies that would come on the screen would have the story of revenge son who is fighting with the whole world to take revenge of his mother or father or lovers death by a cruel man. In some ways these movies were setting a trend that revenge is the way to go or revenge is the best policy, but does the Bible talk about that that revenge is the way to go or the Bible tells us to forgive !

The parable in Matthew 18:23-33 offers profound insights into the importance of forgiveness and the consequences of clinging to unforgiveness. In this story, a servant, forgiven a staggering debt by his master, starkly refuses to extend the same mercy to a fellow servant with a much smaller debt. The master, in response, chastises the unforgiving servant for withholding the mercy he himself had received.

This parable is a poignant reminder that forgiveness is not a one-sided transaction but a reciprocal process. As Jesus emphasized in the Lord's Prayer, "Forgive us our trespasses as we forgive those who trespass against us" (Matthew 6:12). The reciprocity inherent in this prayer underscores a profound truth: to receive forgiveness, we must be willing to extend forgiveness. Clinging to grudges and denying forgiveness serves only to block the flow of mercy into our own lives, hindering the experience of true inner peace.

True forgiveness demands more than a mere verbal expression; it necessitates a forgetting — a conscious decision to release the grip of negative emotions tethered to the hurt. This is not an act of forgetfulness but a deliberate choice to relinquish the power of resentment and move forward with a clean slate. Holding onto pain, nursing grudges, and harboring thoughts of revenge only perpetuate bitterness, causing harm not only to ourselves but also to those around us.

In light of these profound principles, here are five practical steps to achieve complete forgiveness — steps that I have personally experienced and believe can be transformative in your life as well.

1. UNCONDITIONAL FORGIVENESS

The first step towards achieving total forgiveness is to let go of any conditions that we might have attached to our forgiveness. According to 1 John 1:9, God is faithful and just to forgive us without any condition. In the same way, our forgiveness towards others should also be unconditional. This means that we must be willing to forgive regardless of the circumstances or the other person's behavior.

If we keep conditions while forgiving someone, then it's not true forgiveness but rather a compromise. When we attach conditions to our forgiveness, we are essentially saying that the other person must meet certain criteria before we can forgive them. This not only creates a sense of superiority but also prevents us from experiencing true inner peace.

Unconditional forgiveness involves letting go of the need for control and allowing ourselves to be vulnerable. It requires us to trust that God is in control and that He will guide us towards reconciliation and healing. Unconditional forgiveness is the first step towards achieving total forgiveness. It involves letting go of any conditions we might have attached to our forgiveness and trusting in God's guidance towards healing and reconciliation.

2. GO AND ASK FORGIVENESS

The second step towards achieving total forgiveness is to go and ask for forgiveness if we have wronged someone. In the story of The Prodigal Son in Luke 15, we see that the father was actively seeking his son's return, even though his son had wronged him. The father was not sitting at home waiting for his son to come back, but he was out looking for him. This shows us that forgiveness is not about holding back, but it's about taking the high road and taking the extra step towards reconciliation.

When we have wronged someone, it's easy to feel ashamed and embarrassed, and we might be hesitant to reach out to them. However, the act of asking for forgiveness is a humbling experience that allows us to take responsibility for our actions and show genuine remorse for the pain we have caused.

We must not wait for the other person to take the first step towards reconciliation. Instead, we must take the initiative and reach out to them. This shows that we are sincere in our desire for reconciliation and that we are willing to do whatever it takes to make things right.

The second step towards achieving total forgiveness is to take the initiative and go and ask for forgiveness if we have wronged someone. It's about taking the high road, being humble, and taking responsibility for our actions. By doing so, we can show genuine remorse and sincerity in our desire for reconciliation.

3. RECONCILIATION

The third step towards achieving total forgiveness is reconciliation. God is a God of reconciliation, as we see in the story of Adam and Eve in the garden of Eden. Even though they sinned, God did not turn his back on them. Instead, he came down to meet them first (Genesis 3:8-9). Although they were punished, God set up a plan for redemption and reconciliation with the human race (Genesis 3:15).

Not only did God promise reconciliation, but he also fulfilled that promise by sending his only son, Jesus Christ, to save us from our sins. Through Christ's sacrifice on the cross, we have been reconciled with God and have been given the opportunity to be reconciled with others as well.

When we forgive someone, it's not enough to just say the words. We must also take action to restore and reconcile the relationship. This involves putting aside our pride, letting go of the past, and making a genuine effort to rebuild trust and respect.

Reconciliation requires a willingness to listen, understand, and empathize with the other person's feelings and perspectives. It also requires a commitment to forgiveness and a willingness to move forward without holding grudges or resentment.

Just as God went to great lengths to reconcile with us, we must also be willing to go to great lengths to reconcile with others. Through reconciliation, we can experience healing, restoration, and renewed relationships.

The third step towards achieving total forgiveness is reconciliation. We must be willing to take action to restore and reconcile with those we have forgiven, just as God reconciled with us through Christ. Through reconciliation, we can experience healing and renewed relationships.

4. STOP BLAMING GOD

When we experience something disastrous or devastating in our lives, it's easy to fall into the trap of blaming God. However, it's important to understand that God is a loving Father who always has our best interests at heart. Instead of blaming God, we should turn to Him for comfort, guidance, and healing.

Forgiveness is a crucial aspect of our relationship with God, and it can help us to let go of our negative emotions and find healing. When we forgive, we release ourselves from the burden of anger, bitterness, and resentment, and we open ourselves up to God's grace and mercy.

Forgiveness can be a challenging process, especially when we feel hurt or wronged by someone else. However, it's essential to remember that forgiveness is not just about the other person; it's about us and our relationship with God. We must seek forgiveness from God for any wrongdoing on our part, and we must also be willing to forgive others who have hurt us.

When we blame God for our problems or difficulties, we are essentially refusing to forgive Him for allowing these things to happen. However, it's important to remember that God is not the cause of our problems, but rather He allows them to happen for our ultimate good. When we trust in His sovereignty and love, we can find the strength to forgive and move forward with our lives.

We must stop blaming God for everything that happens in our lives, and instead, we must seek His comfort, guidance, and healing. Forgiveness is an essential aspect of our relationship with God and others, and it can help us to let go of our negative emotions and find peace. Let us trust in God's love and sovereignty, and let us seek His forgiveness and offer forgiveness to others as well.

5. FORGIVING YOURSELF

Forgiving ourselves can be one of the most difficult steps in the process of forgiveness. It's easy to blame ourselves for the mistakes we've made and the wrongs we've committed. However, dwelling on our past mistakes and failures can prevent us from moving forward in our lives and reaching our full potential.

We must remember that we are all human, and we all make mistakes. Even the apostle Peter denied Jesus three times, but he was able to seek forgiveness and move forward in his faith. Similarly, if we ask for forgiveness and repent of our wrongs, God is faithful and just to forgive us and cleanse us from all unrighteousness.

The story of Judas Iscariot is a tragic example of someone who couldn't forgive himself and move on from his mistake. He betrayed Jesus and ultimately took his own life out of guilt and shame. However, it's important to remember that God's love and forgiveness are always available to us, no matter what we've done.

When we refuse to forgive ourselves, we are essentially rejecting God's forgiveness and grace. We must learn to let go of our past mistakes and embrace the present moment with God's love and mercy. We can start by acknowledging our mistakes and asking for God's forgiveness, and then we can work on forgiving ourselves and moving forward with the God-given grace.

Forgiving ourselves can be a challenging and difficult process, but it's essential for our spiritual growth and well-being. We must remember that God's love and forgiveness are always available to us, and we can move forward from our mistakes and embrace the present moment with His grace. Let us learn to let go of our past mistakes, forgive ourselves, and live in the freedom and joy of God's love.

FORGIVENESS CHALLENGE

The forgiveness challenge is a powerful way to experience the transformative power of forgiveness in our lives. Forgiveness is not just a one-time event, but a continuous process of letting go of resentment, bitterness, and anger towards others. When we choose to forgive, we free ourselves from the burden of carrying negative emotions and open up our hearts to experience love, joy, and peace.

The first step in the forgiveness challenge is to identify the people in our lives who we hold grudges against. It can be someone who has hurt us in the past, a family member or friend with whom we've had a falling out, or even ourselves for mistakes we've made.

Once we've identified the people we need to forgive, the next step is to take the initiative and reach out to them. This can be a difficult and uncomfortable process, but it's essential for healing and reconciliation. We can start by apologizing for our part in the conflict or hurt and expressing our desire to move forward in a positive direction.

Forgiveness is not about forgetting what happened or excusing the other person's behavior. It's about choosing to let go of our negative emotions towards them and releasing them from our judgment. This doesn't mean that we condone their actions or continue to have a relationship with them, but it does mean that we choose to no longer hold onto our anger or resentment.

Forgiveness is a powerful act of strength and courage. It takes humility to admit our own faults and to reach out to those we've hurt or who have hurt us. When we choose to forgive, we open ourselves up to experiencing God's love and grace, which can bring healing and restoration to our relationships.

In conclusion, the forgiveness challenge is a powerful way to experience the transformative power of forgiveness in our lives. By identifying the people we need to forgive, taking the initiative to reach out to them, and choosing to let go of our negative emotions towards them, we can experience healing, reconciliation, and freedom. Let us embrace the challenge of forgiveness and experience the joy and peace that comes from choosing to forgive and let go.

Chapter 10

Building Christian Families: Biblical Principles of a Family

Family is one of the most beautiful thing that God has designed it is the best way to understand the Godheadship also in our personal life, family a design that can keep you happy, family is a design that can help you grow, family is a design to make your whole. But sadly today in India 4 out of 10 marriages are not working, before few years this was not the scenario, marriages were being taken where is seriously in India were as it is Christian or non-Christian marriages. Marriages in India are really different than the marriages in the western world, marriages in India are usually 3 to 4 days event with more than 1000 people and they are all family and friends, it's really hard for a western person to even imagine what Indian wedding is until and unless they come and experience it by them self it is not a union of just two people it is a union and a bond between two families, two villages, sometimes two states and cultures and that's how it works in India it is not a small gathering of 50 to 100 people it is a witnessing ceremony of more than 1000 people who have come to see this union coming to reality, they are the witness that these two families this to villages will be together forever because most of the time the marriages are fixed by the families or friends and it is called an arranged marriages, but there are pros and cons to the arrange marriage style also because it is fixed sometime just over a cup of tea it can break that easily also. As a pastor I have come across so many stories like that even inside the church that are heartbreaking - domestic violence, verbal abuse, sexual abuse, torture, cases of dowry demand, false cases against the men and so much more, is this the way God intended family to be?

The institution of family is a divine design and purpose of God. It is the foundational unit of society, and it is where individuals learn the basics of love, respect, and responsibility. In the creation account in Genesis, God saw that it was not good for man to be alone, and He provided a companion for Adam. This companion was not just a helper, but someone who would complete him and be his partner in life.

God's plan for the family is clear in the Bible. In Ephesians 5, Paul emphasizes the importance of the marriage relationship, stating that the husband should love his wife as Christ loved the church, and the wife should respect her husband. This relationship is a picture of Christ's love for the church, and it is a beautiful representation of God's plan for humanity.

The family unit is crucial in raising children who will become responsible members of society. Parents are responsible for teaching their children values, morals, and principles that will guide them through life. Children need the guidance and nurturing that only a family can provide. The family is where children learn to love, respect, and serve others, and it is where they learn to be responsible citizens.

Sadly, the family unit is under attack in our society today. Many families are broken, and children are growing up without the guidance and love they need. Divorce, abuse, neglect, and other issues are tearing families apart. It is important for us to recognize the value of the family unit and to do everything we can to protect and strengthen it. God's design for the family is a beautiful and essential part of His plan for humanity. The family is the foundational unit of society, and it is where individuals learn the basics of love, respect, and responsibility. As we strive to protect and strengthen the family, we honor God's plan for our lives and for society as a whole.

God has designed the family to reproduce and multiply, as stated in Genesis 1:27-28. Additionally, God has assigned specific roles and responsibilities to each family member. This design allows for the family to function in a harmonious and cohesive manner. By understanding and fulfilling their respective roles, family members can work together towards a common goal of building a strong and healthy family unit. Ultimately, this supports God's plan for humanity and contributes to a stable and prosperous society.

➢ HUSBAND

Ephesians 5:25-28 "Husbands, love your wives, even as Christ also loved the church, and gave himself for it; That he might sanctify and cleanse it with the washing of water by the word, That he might present it to himself a glorious church, not having spot, or wrinkle, or any such thing; but that it should be holy and without blemish. So ought men to love their wives as their own bodies. He that loveth his wife loveth himself.

As a Christian husband, it is important to understand that your role is not just to provide for your family but also to love and care for your wife as Christ loved the church. Here are some ways to live out this calling in today's situation:

• Love sacrificially: Just as Christ gave himself up for the church, husbands are called to love their wives sacrificially. This means putting their needs before your own and making sacrifices for their well-being.

- Lead spiritually: As the head of the household, husbands have a responsibility to lead their families spiritually. This includes praying together, attending church together, and studying the Bible together.

- Respect your wife: It is important to value and respect your wife as an equal partner in your marriage. Listen to her opinions, honor her feelings, and treat her with dignity and kindness.

- Communicate openly: Communication is key in any relationship, and husbands should strive to communicate openly and honestly with their wives. This means sharing your thoughts and feelings, actively listening to your wife, and working together to resolve any conflicts that arise.

- Be faithful: Just as Christ is faithful to the church, husbands should be faithful to their wives. This includes being emotionally faithful, physically faithful, and avoiding any behaviors or relationships that could jeopardize your marriage.

Remember, being a Christian husband is a lifelong journey of growth and learning. By relying on God's strength and guidance, you can honor Him by loving and caring for your wife in the way He intended.

➢ FATHER

The role of Christian fathers is significant in raising their children:Fathers have the primary responsibility of bringing up their children in the teachings of the Lord (Ephesians 6:4). Fathers should be proactive in their children's spiritual upbringing and set a good example for them to follow.

❖ Fathers should avoid provoking their children to anger or wrath:

❖ Provoking children can lead to discouragement, resentment, and a breakdown in the relationship (Colossians 3:21).

❖ Fathers should refrain from belittling, shaming, or discouraging their children.

❖ Instead, they should provide guidance, love, and support to their children and be a positive influence in their lives.

❖ Bringing up children in the nurture and admonition of the Lord involves teaching them the ways of God:

❖ Fathers should prioritize reading and studying the Bible together, attending church, praying together, and setting an example of Christian living. By doing so, fathers can instill a deep understanding of God's love and grace in their children's hearts and lead them towards a life of faith.

❖ Fathers should recognize their children as individuals with their own personalities and thoughts:Children have unique personalities, gifts, and talents that should be encouraged and developed.

❖ Fathers should avoid trying to mold their children into their own image or forcing them to conform to their expectations.Instead, they should encourage their children to be the best versions of themselves while guiding them towards Christ.

❖ Being a Christian father requires patience, compassion, and a willingness to learn and grow: Fatherhood is a lifelong journey of learning and growth, and it requires a willingness to adapt and change.Fathers should seek out resources and support to help them in their role as spiritual leaders.

By leaning on God's grace and guidance, fathers can fulfill their role as Christian fathers and make a positive impact on their children's lives.

➢ WIFE

As a Christian wife in today's circumstances, there are specific roles and responsibilities that are outlined in the Bible. These roles are meant to promote unity, love, and respect within the marriage. Ephesians 5:22-23 provides guidance for wives and their relationships with their husbands:

1. Submission and Respect:

- Wives are called to submit to their husbands, as unto the Lord (Ephesians 5:22).

- Submission is a voluntary act of respect and trust, recognizing the authority and leadership of the husband in the marriage relationship.

- In addition to submission, wives are also called to show respect towards their husbands (Ephesians 5:33).

- Respect involves acknowledging the value and worth of the husband as a person, and seeking to honor and uplift him in their marriage relationship.

- By showing both submission and respect towards their husbands, wives can create an atmosphere of love, trust, and mutual understanding within their marriage.

2. Husband as the Head of the Household:

- The Bible teaches that the husband is the head of the wife, just as Christ is the head of the church (Ephesians 5:23).

- This means that husbands have the responsibility to lead their wives and families in a way that honors God and promotes love and respect within the home.

- Wives can show respect towards their husbands by trusting their leadership and seeking to be a supportive partner in their marriage.

- Respect also involves listening to and valuing the opinions and perspectives of the husband, even if they may not always agree on everything.

- By showing respect towards their husbands, wives can foster a sense of unity and harmony in their marriage that honors God and strengthens their family.

3. Promoting Unity and Love:

- The ultimate goal of the husband and wife relationship is to promote unity, love, and respect within the marriage (Ephesians 5:28-33).

- Wives can contribute to this goal by showing love, submission, and respect towards their husbands, communicating effectively, and seeking to resolve conflicts in a peaceful manner.

- Respect involves recognizing the strengths and gifts of the husband, and supporting him in using those gifts to serve God and their family.

- By working together with mutual respect and submission out of reverence for Christ (Ephesians 5:21), husbands and wives can create a strong foundation for their marriage and family life.

➢ MOTHER

1. Motherhood as a God-Given Calling:

- In 1 Timothy 5:14, Paul instructs younger women to marry, bear children, and guide the home.

- This passage highlights the importance of motherhood as a calling from God, and encourages women to embrace their role as caretakers and nurturers of their families.

- Being a mother involves not only giving birth to and raising children, but also creating a loving and stable home environment that fosters growth and development for each family member.

2. Love and Respect for Husband and Children:

- Titus 2:4-5 instructs older women to teach younger women to love their husbands and children, to be discreet, chaste, keepers at home, and obedient to their husbands.

- Mothers are called to love their husbands and children sacrificially, modeling Christ's love for his Church.

- This involves being patient, kind, and forgiving towards family members, and making their needs a priority.

- Mothers can also demonstrate respect towards their husbands by listening to their opinions, supporting their decisions, and submitting to their leadership in the home.

- By showing love and respect towards their husbands and children, mothers can create a healthy and supportive family environment that honors God and fosters growth and development.

3. Guiding and Teaching Children:

- Mothers have a significant role in guiding and teaching their children, both through their words and actions.

- This involves modeling Christian values and behaviors, such as honesty, generosity, kindness, and forgiveness.

- Mothers can also teach their children about the Bible and help them develop a personal relationship with God.

- By guiding and teaching their children in the ways of the Lord, mothers can help their children grow into mature and faithful believers.

4. The Importance of Community:

- The passages in 1 Timothy and Titus emphasize the importance of older women teaching and mentoring younger women in the church.

- Mothers can benefit from the wisdom and guidance of older women, and can also offer support and encouragement to other mothers in the church community.

- Being part of a supportive and loving community can help mothers navigate the challenges of motherhood and grow in their faith and relationship with God.

In summary, being a Christian mother involves embracing motherhood as a God-given calling, showing love and respect towards husbands and children, guiding and teaching children in the ways of the Lord, and being part of a supportive community of believers.

➢ CHILDREN

Exodus 20:12 "Honour thy father and thy mother: that thy days may be long upon the land which the LORD thy God giveth thee."

- Children can honor their parents by showing them respect and gratitude. This can be done through actions such as helping with household chores, spending quality time with parents, and expressing appreciation for their support and love.

- It's important to recognize that parents have a unique role in the family and that their guidance and wisdom can be invaluable in navigating life's challenges. By showing respect and honor to parents, children can build a strong foundation for a healthy relationship that lasts beyond childhood and into adulthood.

- The verse also suggests that honoring parents is linked to a long life on earth. While this may not be a guarantee, it highlights the idea that showing respect and honor to parents can lead to a more fulfilling life.

Ephesians 6:1-3 "Children, obey your parents in the Lord: for this is right. Honour thy father and mother; which is the first commandment with promise; That it may be well with thee, and thou mayest live long on the earth."

- Obedience to parents means following their rules and guidelines, which can include things like curfews, homework expectations, and safety precautions. Children who obey their parents demonstrate respect for authority and can develop self-discipline and responsibility.

- However, obedience is not just about following rules blindly. Children can communicate with their parents if they have questions or concerns about rules, and work collaboratively to find solutions that work for everyone involved.

- Honoring parents also means showing respect for their feelings, opinions, and decisions. Even if children do not always agree with their parents, they can listen respectfully and consider their perspective. This can help foster open and honest communication and build a stronger relationship between parents and children.

- The verse suggests that honoring parents is not just a moral obligation, but also has practical benefits. When children honor their parents, they are more likely to have a healthy and prosperous life. This includes building strong relationships with others, making good decisions, and ultimately living a fulfilling life.

➤ SIBLINGS

I Timothy 5:1-3 "Rebuke not an elder, but intreat him as a father; and the younger men as brethren; The elder women as mothers; the younger as sisters, with all purity. Honour widows that are widows indeed."

Paul is teaching Timothy, and us, that a family unit behaves with respect towards one another. In the church we are to respect and honor others as we would our own brothers, sisters, parents and extended family.

As Christian siblings, we are called to treat each other with respect and love, just as we would treat our own family members. This means that we should avoid harsh or judgmental attitudes towards each other, and instead, strive to build each other up and encourage one another in our faith.

In our modern world, it can be easy to fall into the trap of individualism, where we focus only on our own needs and desires, and forget about the needs of our siblings in Christ. However, as Paul reminds us, we are all part of one family, and we should strive to maintain healthy and respectful relationships with each other.

This can mean taking the time to listen to our siblings' concerns and needs, offering a helping hand when needed, and being willing to forgive and reconcile when conflicts arise. We should also honor and respect those who are older and wiser than us, just as we would honor our own parents and elders in our biological families.

Ultimately, as Christian siblings, we are called to reflect the love and unity of our Heavenly Father, and to work together towards building up His Kingdom here on earth.

➤ FAMILY

When we get a grasp of the family structure God has established, we can get a better understanding of how God wants us to interact with one another and with His authority. The family unit points us to another establishment God has ordained—the church. Jesus Christ is the head of the church. He is the authority. The church as a whole is His bride. We as individuals in the church are His children and siblings one with another. If you have a proper family unit, then your children will have a better understanding of God, His church and His authority. If your children never learn to respect their parents, whom they live with and interact with, then how are they going to learn to respect God whom they cannot see? When parents teach their children that there is authority, responsibility and consequences for wrong actions, the children will much more quickly understand who God is and the authority He has in our lives. Do your children a favor and establish a family as God defines it and they will grow up with a better understanding of God and the wonderful salvation He offers?

Here are some additional points to consider:

1. The family unit is the foundation for a healthy society. As we see in the Bible, God established the family as the building block for all other social institutions. When families are strong, society as a whole is strong.

2. The church is also an important part of our lives. It is where we go to worship God, learn more about Him, and fellowship with other believers. As members of the church, we have a responsibility to support and encourage one another.

3. God's authority is something that we must respect and honor. He is the ultimate authority, and everything else in our lives should flow from our relationship with Him. When we submit to God's authority, we are able to experience His blessings and guidance in our lives.

4. As parents, it is our responsibility to teach our children about God's authority and the importance of the family and church. We must model respectful behavior, and teach our children to obey and honor us as their parents. When children learn to respect authority in the family unit, they will be better equipped to understand and submit to God's authority in their lives.

5. Finally, we must remember that our ultimate goal as Christians is to glorify God in all that we do. Whether in the family, the church, or society at large, we should strive to honor God with our words and actions. By doing so, we will be a light to the world and lead others to Christ.

In conclusion, the power of the Christian family cannot be underestimated. God has designed the family structure to be a representation of His love for us and to teach us how to interact with one another and with His authority. A strong and healthy family unit can have a profound impact on the spiritual growth and development of children, leading them to a better understanding of God and His salvation.

It is important for parents to establish a family as God defines it, with love, respect, and a focus on His Word. By doing so, children can learn to honor their parents, respect authority, and develop a strong foundation of faith that will guide them throughout their lives.

As we strive to live as a Christian family, we can also impact the broader church community, serving as an example of God's love and grace. By prioritizing our relationships with God, our spouse, and our children, we can build strong, healthy families that reflect the beauty of God's design and point others to the love of Christ.

Chapter 11

From Death to Life: Exploring the Hope of Resurrection

Death is the most depressing word in the whole world. Death is a big word that leads us to the fear of losing someone forever, it is never easy to say goodbyes. Death always implies separation and the end. I remember during the Covid time in 2021 April there was the death wave of Covid – 19 second wave, everyone was getting affected and there was the news of death everywhere. We were not ready to lose our dear ones and suddenly I lost my dad during this time, I literally didn't know what do to do, as the Church associate pastor I took the charge of the burial and all the other things because my dad was the senior Pastor and he was just gone so I just took the charge led the funeral and burial service just as a pastor would do for any other believers in the church I showed all my strength and courage that day as the Pastor of the church but after everything was done I broke down as a son who had just lost his father. I didn't had any strength or courage anymore, it was so hard that I couldn't visit the place where he died for nearly 3 months. So I know what it really means when we use the word death. But as Christians, we believe that death is not the end. It's just a change of address. Jesus Christ conquered death through his resurrection, and through him, we too have the hope of eternal life. The power of resurrection is central to the Christian faith and is what gives us comfort and hope in the face of death.

Death is a part of life, but it is not the end. For believers, it is a transition from this earthly life to an eternal life with God. Through Jesus' death and resurrection, we have been reconciled to God and given the opportunity to experience the joy and peace of eternal life with Him.

In the face of death, Christians can take comfort in knowing that death has no power over us. We have the hope of resurrection and eternal life because of what Jesus has done for us. This hope can sustain us in the midst of grief and loss and give us the strength to face even the most difficult circumstances.

As we navigate the challenges of life and face the reality of death, let us hold fast to the hope of resurrection and the promise of eternal life. Let us also remember that Jesus' resurrection is not just a future hope, but a present reality that can transform our lives here and now. By placing our trust in Jesus, we can experience the power of resurrection in our daily lives and be a witness to the hope that is found in Him.

As Christians, death is not the end, but a transition from this life to the next. Death is the separation of the body and the spirit, and it is something that we all must face eventually. However, as believers, we have hope and confidence in the promise of eternal life through Jesus Christ. First, it is important to understand that death was not God's original plan for humanity. In the beginning, God created Adam and Eve to live forever in perfect communion with Him. But sin entered the world through their disobedience, and death became a reality for all of us (Romans 5:12). However, God did not leave us without hope. Through His Son, Jesus Christ, He provided a way for us to be reconciled to Him and to have eternal life (John 3:16).

As believers, we can take comfort in the fact that death is not the end, but a new beginning. Paul tells us in 1 Corinthians 15:51-55 that when Christ returns, we will be transformed and our mortal bodies will be replaced with glorified bodies that will never die. Death will be swallowed up in victory, and we will have eternal life with our Lord and Savior.

So how should we deal with death as Christians? We should grieve and mourn for our loved ones who have passed away, but we should also take comfort in the hope of eternal life. We can trust that God is sovereign and in control, even in the midst of our grief. We can also draw near to Him in prayer and seek comfort in His Word.

Jesus Himself wept at the death of His friend Lazarus, even though He knew that He would soon raise him from the dead (John 11:35). This shows us that it is okay to grieve and feel the pain of loss, but we must not lose sight of the hope that we have in Christ. Death is not the end for believers in Christ. It is a transition from this life to the next, and we can have confidence in the promise of eternal life. As we grieve the loss of our loved ones, we can turn to God for comfort and strength, knowing that He is with us and will never leave us.

The power of resurrection for a believer is a central and foundational truth of the Christian faith. The resurrection of Jesus Christ from the dead is the ultimate demonstration of God's power and victory over sin, death, and the devil. It is the hope of eternal life for all who put their trust in Him. The power of resurrection for a believer is multifaceted and life-changing. The resurrection of Jesus Christ is the cornerstone of the Christian faith and has tremendous implications for believers both in this life and in the next.

Here are some ways in which the power of resurrection is important for a believer:

1. Victory over sin and death: Through the resurrection of Jesus Christ, believers have victory over sin and death. Romans 6:4 says, "We were buried therefore with him by baptism into death, in order that, just as Christ was raised from the dead by the glory of the Father, we too might walk in newness of life." Because of Christ's resurrection, believers are no longer slaves to sin and death, but are freed to live in newness of life.

2. Hope for eternal life: The resurrection of Jesus Christ gives believers hope for eternal life. 1 Peter 1:3 says, "Blessed be the God and Father of our Lord Jesus Christ! According to his great mercy, he has caused us to be born again to a living hope through the resurrection of Jesus Christ from the dead." Believers can look forward to eternal life with Christ because of his victory over death.

3. Power for daily living: The power of resurrection is not just for the afterlife, but also for daily living. Ephesians 1:19-20 says, "And what is the immeasurable greatness of his power toward us who believe, according to the working of his great might that he worked in Christ when he raised him from the dead." The same power that raised Christ from the dead is available to believers to help them live a life of faith and obedience.

4. Assurance of salvation: The power of resurrection provides assurance of salvation for believers. Romans 8:11 says, "If the Spirit of him who raised Jesus from the dead dwells in you, he who raised Christ Jesus from the dead will also give life to your mortal bodies through his Spirit who dwells in you." The presence of the Holy Spirit in a believer's life is evidence of their salvation and gives them the assurance that they will also be raised to eternal life.

In summary, the power of resurrection for a believer is multifaceted, providing victory over sin and death, hope for eternal life, power for daily living, and assurance of salvation.

Chapter 12

The Joy of Giving: Unleashing the Power of Generosity

Giving is an integral part of the Christian life, reflecting our gratitude to God for all He has given us and our love for our neighbors. The act of giving in a Christian life is not merely a duty or obligation, but a joyful response to God's grace and provision. This is very personal for me as I have seen this more than I have read about it. My father was born in a very poor family in the small town called Balangir in the western part of Odisha. Their family had 10 siblings in total and when he was in his teenages he lost his father and the family was left with 7 sisters and 3 brother with a not so educated widow who then had to sale vegetables and sometime bangles just for the survival of all these people at home. Many times they didn't had the second meal of the day at their home to just eat. So my dad had to work from a very young age just for the survival of his family. God helped them survived their lives and then God help them establish for good, my dad had a great business where he was able to make really good money but then he received the calling of God in his life and he left everything that he had to went for ministry. He started working for the Lord with real hardships because now he was working for a mission and in India when you are working for a mission you should not expect a lot of salary it's really different from the West, you will be surprised that some people in India are doing Ministries getting a salary are they call honorarium of ₹300 every month that is not even $5, but they are the most faithful people you will ever meet because they are not in the Ministries because they will get status or they will get money or they will get anything else they are simply here to serve the Lord with everything they got and they can. And my father started like that as well in a very less honorarium he started working for a mission as an accountant he was really faithful in his calling we used to live in a one room house and it was enough for us even though it wasn't. He followed the Lord with all his heart and worked for his kingdom and then the Lord called him to start a small orphanage, so he left that account in Job and we moved to a different city and he started a small orphanage in our home with 30 kids, this was the most daring step he ever took in his entire life without no support and without any surety he started this orphanage, it was really difficult to see what he had to go through to fulfil the calling of the Lord in his life, I was a child but I was understanding everything that he was doing for the calling in his life, my parents came together and followed the calling of the Lord in their lives and through their life they even sold their wedding rings and all the other jewelleries they had just to feed this children, it was really challenging for them but in what so ever situation they never stop doing it for the kingdom of God. By seeing their hardship in the struggle I decided in my life that I never wanted to join Ministry because it's a lot to do but the Lords will watch something else and today I am in Ministry and I don't know what else could I have been if I was not in Ministries, I think this is the best decision of my life that I have taken to follow the Lord with all my heart and with all I have. Their life taught me how to give and be happy at the same time, They did not had much but did it had enough, but did not have everything in our house but we had everything that we need. Through their lives they have impacted more than 500 children's life and given them a bright future. And that's were I learned how to give, I remember when I graduated from the BIBLE school in 2011 one of a mission wanted to support me for my work and they started paying me ₹4500 ($56) every month as a support or as an honorarium because I was bought up by this wonderful couple my parents I did what they did for their whole life, I added two Evangelist with me to fulfil the calling in my life and I used to pay them 1500 ($18) each and then I would be left with 1500 for myself, from there I would pay my tight and the rest of the money would be used for my day to day life needs, but it was never too less for me because I saw what that small amount that I was investing in the kingdom of God was doing. Even today this has become my lifestyle that I spent more than 70% of my earning for the kingdom of God, today the Lord has help me to pioneered and established more than 35 churches and I teach all my pastors and leaders the same to give for the kingdom of God.

Through giving, we can demonstrate our faith in God's promises, and share His love and compassion with those around us. Whether we give of our time, talents, or resources, we are called to be generous, cheerful, and sacrificial in our giving, seeking to bless others and bring glory to God. By giving, we can participate in God's work in the world, helping to alleviate suffering, promote justice, and share the good news of the Gospel.

As a Christian, giving is important for several reasons. Here are some Bible verses that explain why:

1. Giving is an act of worship: "Honor the Lord with your wealth, with the firstfruits of all your crops" (Proverbs 3:9). Giving is a way to honor God and acknowledge that all we have comes from Him.

2. Giving helps those in need: "Whoever is generous to the poor lends to the Lord, and he will repay him for his deed" (Proverbs 19:17). Giving enables us to help those who are less fortunate and demonstrate Christ's love to them.

3. Giving demonstrates faith: "Each of you should give what you have decided in your heart to give, not reluctantly or under compulsion, for God loves a cheerful giver" (2 Corinthians 9:7). Giving demonstrates our faith in God's provision and our willingness to trust Him with our resources.

4. Giving brings blessings: "Give, and it will be given to you. A good measure, pressed down, shaken together and running over, will be poured into your lap. For with the measure you use, it will be measured to you" (Luke 6:38). When we give generously, God promises to bless us in return.

Giving is an important aspect of the Christian life. It helps us demonstrate our love for God and our neighbours, and it brings blessings to both the giver and the receiver.

The power of giving for God's Kingdom lies in its ability to transform lives, both of the giver and the recipient. When we give sacrificially and generously, we participate in God's work in the world, demonstrating His love and compassion to those around us. Our giving can help meet the physical, emotional, and spiritual needs of others, and can bring hope and healing to those who are hurting.

Moreover, giving can have a transformative effect on our own hearts and minds, drawing us closer to God and deepening our faith. By giving, we can cultivate a spirit of generosity and gratitude, and learn to trust God more fully with our resources and our lives. As we give, we can experience the joy and fulfilment that come from serving others and making a positive difference in the world.

Ultimately, the power of giving lies in its ability to advance God's Kingdom on earth, spreading the Gospel message and building up His church. Through our giving, we can support missionaries, fund evangelistic initiatives, and contribute to the work of local churches and ministries. By partnering with God in this way, we can have a lasting impact on the lives of others and help bring about His Kingdom on earth.

The power of giving for God's Kingdom:

• Transforming Lives: Giving has the power to transform lives, both of the giver and the recipient. It can help meet the physical, emotional, and spiritual needs of others, bringing hope and healing to those who are hurting.

• Deepening Our Faith: Giving can deepen our faith and draw us closer to God. It can cultivate a spirit of generosity and gratitude, and help us trust God more fully with our resources and our lives.

• Spreading the Gospel: Through our giving, we can support missionaries, fund evangelistic initiatives, and contribute to the work of local churches and ministries. By partnering with God in this way, we can help spread the Gospel message and build up His church.

• Advancing God's Kingdom: Giving is a way to advance God's Kingdom on earth, making a positive difference in the lives of others and contributing to the work of God in the world.

- Bringing Joy and Fulfilment: Giving can bring joy and fulfilment to our own lives, as we serve others and make a positive impact in the world.

- Obeying God's Commands: Giving is also a way to obey God's commands and demonstrate our love and gratitude to Him. In the Bible, God commands us to be generous and to care for the poor and needy.

Overall, the power of giving for God's Kingdom is multifaceted, encompassing spiritual, emotional, and practical benefits for both the giver and the recipient. Through our giving, we can participate in God's work in the world and help bring about His Kingdom on earth.

In conclusion, the power of giving in a Christian life is immense. Giving allows us to demonstrate our love and gratitude to God, participate in His work in the world, and bring hope and healing to those around us. It can deepen our faith, cultivate a spirit of generosity and gratitude, and bring joy and fulfillment to our own lives. Through our giving, we can advance God's Kingdom on earth, spreading the Gospel message and building up His church. Giving is not just a duty or obligation, but a joyful response to God's grace and provision. As we give sacrificially and generously, we can experience the transformative power of God's love and make a positive difference in the world.

Chapter 13

A Glimpse of the Eternal Home: The Biblical Vision of the Future

As Christians, our faith is anchored in the profound belief that God's love extends not only to humanity but to the entirety of His creation. This divine affection is palpable in the Genesis narrative, where God, after creating light, the sky, land, and sea, declared each element as "good" (Gen 1:4, 12, 18, 21, 25, 31). This underscores God's deep care and immense value for every facet of His creation.

Our Christian hope extends beyond the present, eagerly anticipating the fulfillment of Jesus' promise—a new heaven and a new earth (2 Peter 3:13; Revelation 21:1). This eschatological anticipation is more than a mere theological concept; it is a beacon guiding our faith, reminding us that God is sovereign and trustworthy, actively working out His divine plans for the world.

In light of these foundational beliefs, our attitude toward the earth is not one of indifference. The Bible, as our guide, emphasizes that the earth belongs to the Lord (Psalm 24:1). As faithful stewards, we are entrusted with the responsibility to care for God's creation, recognizing that we are caretakers rather than owners. This stewardship necessitates a commitment to manage the earth responsibly and sustainably.

Additionally, the principle in Luke 15:31 resonates with our role as God's children and stewards. Whatever belongs to the Father is entrusted to His faithful sons and daughters. Consequently, we bear the responsibility to care for the earth with the same love and respect that God demonstrates. This involves taking deliberate actions to protect the environment, conserve natural resources, and minimize waste and pollution.

Allow me to illustrate this principle with a personal testimony. One of my dear friends and brothers in Christ, Jeremy Lowe from the U.S., embarked on a mission trip to India in 2014. During our travels, enjoying some snacks and cola in the car, I thoughtlessly opened the window and casually discarded a cola can. Jeremy, witnessing this act, posed a poignant question, "Do you love your country?" My proud affirmation was met with a gentle rebuke as he remarked, "Yeah, I just saw how much you love your country." This moment of conviction served as a catalyst for change in my behavior. Since then, I have refrained from such actions, remaining inside the car and raising awareness among others about the importance of responsible stewardship.

In essence, our attitude toward the earth is a reflection of our gratitude for God's creation and a demonstration of our commitment to fulfill the stewardship role entrusted to us. By aligning our actions with God's call to care for His creation, we not only honor our divine responsibility but contribute to the well-being of the planet and its inhabitants.

Psalm 115:16 states, "The highest heavens belong to the Lord, but the earth he has given to mankind." This verse highlights the fact that God has entrusted the earth to humanity, giving us the responsibility to care for it and manage its resources wisely.

At the same time, it is important to note that the earth still ultimately belongs to God, as Psalm 24:1 affirms: "The earth is the Lord's, and everything in it, the world, and all who live in it." As stewards of the earth, we are accountable to God for how we use and manage His creation.

Moreover, the fact that God has given the earth to humanity is not a license to exploit or abuse it. Rather, we are called to exercise responsible stewardship, caring for the environment and using its resources in a sustainable and ethical manner.

Taking care of the earth is a responsibility that falls upon all of us. As human beings, we have been given the dominion over the earth by God. However, this dominion should not be seen as a license for destructive domination, but rather as a call to responsible stewardship. Our care for the environment should reflect our love and reverence for the Creator who made it.

To take care of the earth, we must respect nature as a gift from God, but not worship it as if it were God. We should recognize that all of creation was made by God and is therefore precious and worthy of care. Our actions should reflect our gratitude for this gift, and we should be mindful of our impact on the environment.

Our work should not be separate from our worship, but rather an expression of it. Our care for the environment should reflect our love for the Creator and our desire to honor Him. We should strive to be good stewards of the earth, using its resources wisely and caring for it in a way that honors God.

1. Respect nature as a gift from God, but do not worship it as if it were God.

2. See the dominion given to us by God as responsible stewardship, not destructive domination.

3. Recognize that God has given us the responsibility to work and take care of the earth.

4. Strive to maintain the balance of nature and prevent the degradation of the environment.

5. Use the earth's resources in a responsible way, being mindful of our impact on the environment.

6. Our care for the environment should reflect our love for the Creator and our desire to honor Him.

7. Our work should be an expression of our worship, and our care for the environment should be a reflection of our love for the Creator.

8. Remember that taking care of the earth is not just a matter of personal responsibility, but a spiritual one as well.

As Christians, we believe that this earthly life is temporary, and we have a blessed assurance of eternal life in heaven. The Bible tells us that when we accept Jesus Christ as our Lord and Savior, we are saved by grace through faith, and our names are written in the book of life. This means that we have the assurance of eternal life with God in heaven.

In John 14:2-3, Jesus said, "In my Father's house are many rooms; if it were not so, I would have told you. I am going there to prepare a place for you. And if I go and prepare a place for you, I will come back and take you to be with me that you also may be where I am."

This passage tells us that Jesus is preparing a place for us in heaven, and one day He will come back to take us there. Our eternal home is not just a physical place, but a spiritual one. It is a place where we will be with God, and where there will be no more pain, suffering, or tears.

Revelation 21:3-4 says, "And I heard a loud voice from the throne saying, 'Look! God's dwelling place is now among the people, and he will dwell with them. They will be his people, and God himself will be with them and be their God. He will wipe every tear from their eyes. There will be no more death or mourning or crying or pain, for the old order of things has passed away.'"

This is the blessed assurance that we have as Christians - that we have an eternal home with God where we will experience joy, peace, and love forever. And because of this assurance, we can live our lives with purpose and meaning, knowing that our ultimate hope is not in this world, but in the world to come.

The Bible gives us some glimpses and hints about what our eternal home, heaven, will be like for those who believe in Jesus. While we do not have a comprehensive picture of heaven, we can rely on the Scriptures to understand what we can expect.

1. Heaven is a place where we will be with God. In John 14:3, Jesus promised that He would come back to take us to be with Him. In Revelation 21:3, it says, "Behold, the dwelling place of God is with man. He will dwell with them, and they will be his people, and God himself will be with them as their God." Being in the presence of God and having an intimate relationship with Him is the ultimate fulfilment of our deepest longing and desire.

2. Heaven is a place of joy and happiness. In Revelation 21:4, it says, "He will wipe away every tear from their eyes, and death shall be no more, neither shall there be mourning, nor crying, nor pain anymore, for the former things have passed away." Being in

heaven means that we will experience eternal joy and happiness without any hindrance.

3. Heaven is a place of perfect peace. In Revelation 21:27, it says, "Nothing impure will ever enter it, nor will anyone who does what is shameful or deceitful, but only those whose names are written in the Lamb's book of life." The absence of sin, death, and evil means that we will experience perfect peace and rest.

4. Heaven is a place of worship and fellowship. In Revelation 7:9-10, it describes a great multitude of people from every nation, tribe, people, and language who are standing before the throne and worshipping God together. We will also have the opportunity to fellowship with other believers from all over the world who have gone before us.

5. Heaven is a place of eternal life. In John 3:16, it says, "For God so loved the world, that he gave his only Son, that whoever believes in him should not perish but have eternal life." Being in heaven means that we will never die and that we will enjoy eternal life with God and other believers.

We believe that our ultimate destination is heaven, and therefore, we should live our lives with an eternal perspective. Living a preparatory life for heaven means that we live our lives on earth in a way that is consistent with the values, principles, and teachings of Jesus Christ.

Here are some ways in which we can live a heavenly life while on earth:

1. Prioritize our relationship with God: We can prioritize our relationship with God by seeking to know Him more intimately through prayer, reading the Bible, and attending church regularly.

We should also seek to live a life that is pleasing to Him by obeying His commandments and following His teachings.

2. Love and serve others: Jesus taught that the greatest commandment is to love God and love others. We can live a heavenly life by serving others, putting their needs before our own, and showing them the same love and grace that God has shown us.

3. Practice forgiveness and reconciliation: We can live a heavenly life by practicing forgiveness and reconciliation with others. This means that we are willing to forgive those who have wronged us, seek forgiveness when we have wronged others, and work towards reconciliation whenever possible.

4. Be generous and compassionate: We can live a heavenly life by being generous with our time, talents, and resources, and by showing compassion to those who are hurting, marginalized, or in need.

5. Avoid sin and temptation: We can live a heavenly life by avoiding sin and temptation, recognizing that our actions have consequences and that they can have an impact on our relationship with God and others.

6. Share the good news of Jesus Christ: We can live a heavenly life by sharing the good news of Jesus Christ with others, telling them about the hope and salvation that is available to them through faith in Him.

By living a heavenly life while on earth, we can prepare ourselves for the eternal life that awaits us in heaven. We can be confident in the knowledge that our life on earth has a purpose and that we are called to live it in a way that honors God and prepares us for our ultimate destination.

www.ingramcontent.com/pod-product-compliance
Lightning Source LLC
LaVergne TN
LVHW061614070526
838199LV00078B/7281